Jean Parkman Brown

Intervals, Chords and Ear Training for Young Pianoforte

Students

Jean Parkman Brown

Intervals, Chords and Ear Training for Young Pianoforte Students

ISBN/EAN: 9783744783897

Printed In Europe, USA, Canada, Australia, Japan

Cover: Foto ©Thomas Meinert / pixelio.de

More available books at **www.hansebooks.com**

INTERVALS, CHORDS

AND

EAR TRAINING

FOR

YOUNG PIANOFORTE STUDENTS

BY

JEAN PARKMAN BROWN

BOSTON
OLIVER DITSON COMPANY

NEW YORK
CHAS. H. DITSON & CO.

CHICAGO
LYON & HEALY

MADE IN U. S. A.

The most important thing is to cultivate the sense of hearing. Take pains early to distinguish tones and keys by the ear. The bell, the window-pane, the cuckoo,— seek to find what tones they each give out. — ROBERT SCHUMANN.

NOTE BY THE AUTHOR.

I have pursued the course set forth in this book with pupils of various ages. Sometimes, however, with a very young pupil I have found it better not to attempt, the first year, to teach more of the course than is given in the following chapters:

These chapters will give the pupil a thorough knowledge of the major and minor scales, and the primary triads of the major and minor keys. In my own experience in teaching I have found that it has taken the average pupil two or three years to take the entire course.

TABLE OF CONTENTS.

INTRODUCTION.

It is often noticeable how deficient musicians are in knowledge of their art, and how untrained their ears are in the power to follow intelligently harmonic progressions. Even an accurate knowledge of the more common intervals such as major and minor thirds, augmented fifths, diminished sevenths, etc., is by no means common. Nothing is more valuable to the musician, be he composer, teacher, or executant, than some degree of "inner hearing," i.e., the power to feel accurately the correspondence between the note, the written symbol, and the outward effect—the sound; so that if one is asked to sing a minor third or a major seventh, it can be easily done; or so that the same intervals may be instantly recognized when played.

The author of this little book, feeling that children can't begin too early to have their ears properly trained, has compiled a simple and yet thorough set of exercises and examples in rudimentary harmony. Far too much attention has hitherto been given to the mere playing of music, whereas a simple study of harmony and the cultivation of the ear should always go hand in hand with the training of the fingers. A faithful use of this book with even very young children who have a natural love for music will greatly broaden their knowledge, and so will raise the standard of musical intelligence among the public at large.

W. R. SPALDING,

INSTRUCTOR OF HARMONY IN HARVARD UNIVERSITY.

CAMBRIDGE,
   August, 1897.

INTERVALS, CHORDS,

AND

EAR TRAINING.

CHAPTER I.

Tones.

A **tone** is a sound in which pitch is perceptible. The height or depth of a tone is called the pitch of a tone.

Play : 1.

The pitch of D is higher than the pitch of C; the pitch of E is higher than that of D. The pitch of C is lower than that of E.

Play a tone that has a higher pitch than E; play a tone that has a lower pitch than C.

The building material of music consists of **seven fundamental tones** which you hear when you strike the white keys of the piano from C to the C an octave (eight tones) above,

2.

and of the **five tones** lying between these, that you hear when you play the black keys between C and D, D and E, F and G, G and A, A and B, making altogether **twelve tones**. These tones can be repeated in higher and lower octaves.

For example, say "book" in as high a voice as you can; s

" book " in as deep a voice as you can ; say " book " in your natural voice ; you have always said " book," but in different voices.
So the piano can say C in many different voices.   How many
different C's, counting from the lowest to the highest, can you
play on the piano?   You have each time played the tone C, only
sometimes higher, sometimes lower.   Wherever you play on the
keyboard D or E or F, or any one of the twelve tones, you will
be playing D or E or F, or one of the twelve tones, sometimes higher, sometimes lower.

The name of the octave from middle C to the C an octave
higher is the **one-lined** octave, the octaves above are the **two-,
three-,** and **four-lined** octaves.   The octaves below the one-lined
octave are the **small** octave, the **large** octave, and the **contra**
octave.

If you should get a letter from a friend saying he had heard
ġ sung beautifully, by a famous tenor, this small ḡ, with one
line over it, would mean that it was the g in the **one-lined** octave.   Now, some one writes to you that he has at last heard
a cuckoo bird's note, it is ḡ̄, ē̄ ; this small ḡ̄ and ē̄ with two lines

over them are in the **two-lined** octave.   Some opera singers can sing $\overline{\overline{d}}$ and even $\overline{\overline{e}}$; $\overline{\overline{\overline{d}}}$ and $\overline{\overline{\overline{c}}}$ with three lines over them are in the **three-lined** octave.   A tone in the **four-lined** octave is represented by a small letter, as $\overline{\overline{\overline{\overline{e}}}}$ with four lines over it.

A tone in the **small** octave is represented by a small letter with no line over it.   This e is played in the small octave.   A tone in the **large** octave is represented by a large letter.   This E is played in the large octave.   A tone in the **contra** octave is represented by a large letter with one line over it.   This $\overline{E}$ with one line over it, is played in the contra octave.

Play : $\overline{c}$, $\overline{\overline{d}}$, $\overline{G}$,   g, $\overline{\overline{f}}$, $\overline{\overline{\overline{d}}}$,   A,   a, $\overline{b}$.

The smallest distance between tones is a half step.   The next smallest distance is a whole step.   **Play** : ____.   This is a whole step ; from C to the tone produced by playing the black key between it and D is a half step.   Two half steps make a whole step.   **Play** : ____.   This is a whole step ; from E to F ____ is a half step ; from E to the tone you hear when you play the black key next to F is a whole step.

Play a tone that is a half step higher than D.
Play a tone that is a half step higher than E.
Play a tone that is a half step higher than C.
Play a tone that is a whole step higher than G.
Play a tone that is a whole step higher than F.
Play a tone that is a whole step higher than A.
Play a tone that is a half step lower than C.
Play a tone that is a half step lower than B.
Play a tone that is a whole step lower than C.
Play a tone that is a whole step lower than F.
Play a tone that is a whole step lower than D.

Exercise in Ear Training.

Put the pupil where he cannot see the keyboard ; play a tone ; let the pupil tell you the octave it is in, and then try to strike it on the keyboard.   I have had two pianos when I have used this exercise, and have had to repeat generally many times the tone on one piano before the pupil could strike it on the other.

Play in succession tones that are a whole and a half step apart.

Thus :

Let the pupil distinguish between them ; then play separately tones a whole or a half step apart and let the pupil try to tell you which you have played.

REMARK. — Throughout the book the exercises in ear training must be left to the teacher's discretion ; they are mere hints which the teacher must use according to the pupil's ability. Singing is now well taught in many schools, and is probably the best method of cultivating the ear ; but it is essential that when a pupil takes up the study of the piano, his ear should at the same time be trained, as far as possible, to recognize the tones, intervals, and chords of his instrument.

CHAPTER II.

The Major Scale.

Play : c̄,   d̄,   ē,   f̄,   ḡ,   ā,   b̄,   c̿.

This succession of eight tones is the **major scale**. The eighth tone of the scale is the repetition of the first tone an octave higher. In German a scale is called a *Tonleiter* (tone ladder). The successive tones are also called degrees of the scale and are numbered accordingly. The first tone is the first degree, the second tone is the second degree, etc.

Major Scale.

There is a whole step between all the degrees except between the third and the fourth, and the seventh and the eighth. Between each of these there is a half step. We can make this succession of tones, this ladder of tones, beginning on any key of the keyboard, that is, from any pitch. Begin on D.

How far must it be from the first to the second degree? *A whole step.* (**Strike** it.)

How far must it be from the second to the third degree? *A whole step.* (**Strike** it.)

How far must it be from the third to the fourth degree? *A half step.* (**Strike** it.)

How far must it be from the fourth to the fifth degree? *A whole step.* (**Strike** it.)

How far must it be from the fifth to the sixth degree? *A whole step.* (**Strike** it.)

How far must it be from the sixth to the seventh degree? A *whole step.* (**Strike** it.)

How far must it be from the seventh to the eighth degree?
A half step.   (**Strike it.**)

Form the major scale from G, A, E, B. Form it from each one
of the twelve tones.
Learn to say the order of succession of the major scale for-
ward and backward. Thus:
From the first to the second tone is a whole step.
From the second to the third tone, a whole step.
From the third to the fourth tone, a half step, etc.

The name of the first tone of the scale is the **tonic**. The tonic
is the most important tone of the scale.

The name of the fifth tone of the scale is the **dominant**. Dominant means ruling; the fifth tone of the scale is the tone that
dominates or rules the key, and is therefore called the dominant.

The name of the fourth tone of the scale is the **subdominant**.
Sub means under; the fourth tone is the tone below the dominant, it is therefore called the subdominant.[*]

The name of the seventh tone of the scale is the **leading tone**.
The seventh is called the leading tone because it leads a half step
upwards to the tonic of the scale. You hear this if you play the
major scale and stop on the seventh tone.

Play :   5.

How disappointing this is ! Your ear is not satisfied till the
tonic of the scale has been played.

Strike the tonic of the scale of G.
Strike the tonic of the scale of F.
Strike the tonic of the scale of D.
Strike the dominant of the scale of C, of F, of E, of A, of B, of

---

[*] Many authorities have it that the subdominant or lower dominant is so
called because it is the same distance from the tonic in descending as the dominant is from the tonic in ascending.

D, of G. Strike the dominant of the scale beginning on the black key next to C. Strike the dominant of other scales.

Strike the subdominant of C, G, B, E, A. Strike the subdominant of other scales.

Strike the leading tone of E, G, F, C, D. Strike the leading tone of other scales.

Strike the tonic of the scales of which G, D, E, B, C, A, are the dominant.

Strike the tonic of the scales of which G, D, E, A, C, B, are the subdominant.

Strike the tonic of the scales of which G, D, E, B, C, A, are the leading tone.

Exercise in Ear Training.

Place the pupil where he cannot see the keyboard. Play scales slowly, correctly, and incorrectly; the pupil must stop you when you play wrong.

CHAPTER III.

Perfect and Major Intervals.

The distance between two tones is an **interval**.

The interval from the first to the second tone of the major scale is the interval of a **second**.

From the first to the third tone of the major scale is the interval of a **third**.

From the first to the fourth tone of the major scale is the interval of a **fourth**.

From the first to the fifth tone of the major scale is the interval of a **fifth**.

From the first to the sixth tone of the major scale is the interval of a **sixth**.

From the first to the seventh tone of the major scale is the interval of a **seventh**.

From the first to the eighth tone of the major scale is the interval of an **octave**.

Prime is the name given to a unison, see Example 6. If you should sing c̄ and some one else should sing c̄, you would be singing in unison, you would be singing a prime. A prime is written by two notes of the same name, representing the same pitch. The intervals of the major scale reckoned from the tonic are called **normal intervals**.

These intervals are divided into two kinds, **perfect intervals** and **major intervals**.

The **perfect** intervals are the prime (unison), the fourth, the fifth, and the octave.

Perfect Intervals.

The **major** intervals are the second, the third, the sixth, and the seventh.

Major Intervals.

Intervals of a ninth, tenth, eleventh, and twelfth are intervals reckoned from the tonic of the major scale to the repetition of the second, third, fourth, and fifth tones of the scale an octave higher.

The tones that form each of the different intervals can be struck together or in succession. For instance, a perfect fifth can be played ♪ or ♪ .

Remember — this is very important — that the intervals of the major scale, reckoned from the tonic, are perfect or major, and that from these two kinds of intervals, perfect and major, all other intervals are formed.

Write out in a blank harmony book the scale of C, marking the whole and the half steps, and the perfect and the major intervals of the key, reckoned from the tonic, as shown on page 91.[*]

---

* The pupil should reserve in his blank harmony book an entire page for each key.

Exercise in Ear Training.

Place the pupil where he cannot see the keyboard. Try to teach him to recognize by ear the intervals in Examples 7 and 8. Play the perfect prime and the perfect fifth in succession.

Tell the pupil what intervals you have played, and let him distinguish between them ; do the same with the perfect fourth and the perfect fifth :

then play the perfect octave and the perfect fourth.   Play other combinations of perfect intervals till the pupil can distinguish between the perfect intervals ; then play the perfect intervals separately till the pupil can recognize them all.   Then treat the major intervals in the same way.   Play perfect and major intervals in succession, until the pupil can recognize any interval given in Examples 7 and 8, when it is struck separately.

If the pupil has not a quick ear, let him distinguish at first between the major second and perfect fifth, the major seventh and perfect fourth, etc.

Strike each interval simultaneously and successively, that the pupil may learn to recognize the intervals when they are played either way.

CHAPTER IV.

Signature.

This sign ♯ is called a sharp, and when it is placed before a note it means that the note is to be played a half step higher.

This sign ♭ is called a flat, and when it is placed before a note it means that the note is to be played a half step lower.

This sign × is called a double sharp, and when it is placed before a note it means that the note is to be played a whole step higher.

This sign ♭♭ is called a double flat, and when it is placed before a note it means that the note is to be played a whole step lower.

This sign ♮ is called a natural, and when it is placed before a note it means that the note, having been previously raised by a ♯ or lowered by a ♭, is to be played as it was before the sharp or flat was added.

Play: F♯, G♯, A♯, B♭, B♯, C♯, C♭.

Play: . d̿♯ and e̿♭ are enharmonic, that is they are the same tone.

Play: . f̄♯ and ḡ♭ are enharmonic.

Play: . ä♯ and b̄♭ are enharmonic.

We say that c̄♯ and d̄♭ are the same tone.

They are exactly the same tone on the piano, but a singer, a violin or a cello player, or whoever plays an instrument that can make a difference between the two tones, would play

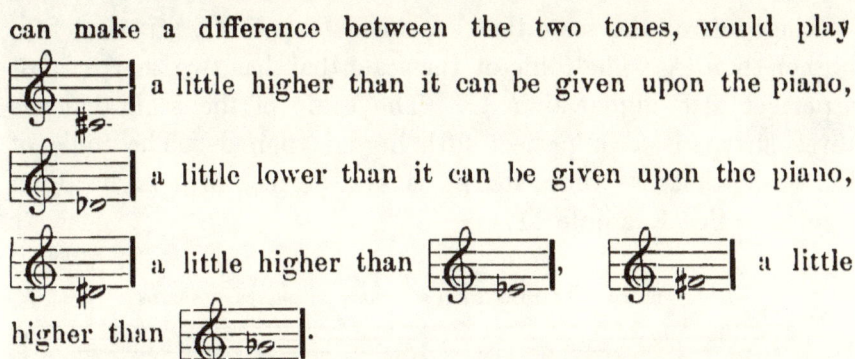 a little higher than it can be given upon the piano,

a little lower than it can be given upon the piano,

a little higher than ⟨⟩, ⟨⟩ a little

higher than ⟨⟩.

A note with a sharp before it is a little nearer the note above than the piano can give it. A note with a flat before it is a little nearer the note below than the piano can give it. Ask a violin player to play ⟨⟩ and ⟨⟩ for you. If you listen very attentively, you will hear a shade of difference between the two tones.

In the writing of seven scales, sharps are required.

The seven successive tones of the major scale must be written by **seven successive notes** — these notes must be raised and lowered as required by sharps or flats; no note must be repeated or skipped. Play the scale beginning on $\bar{\bar{g}}$. The seventh tone is produced by striking the black key between $\bar{\bar{f}}$ and $\bar{\bar{g}}$; this tone is a half step higher than $\bar{\bar{f}}$, therefore $\bar{\bar{f}}\sharp$, and is written ⟨⟩. It must not be written ⟨⟩, though the tone would be the same for the seventh note from $\bar{\bar{g}}$, $f\sharp$ must not be skipped.

Good.   Bad.

10.

The tonics of the scales with sharps are to be found upwards, from C, a perfect fifth apart.

The tonic of the scale that has one sharp is G, a perfect fifth higher than C. The tonic of the scale that has two sharps is d, a perfect fifth higher than G. The tonic of the scale that has three sharps is a, a perfect fifth higher than d. The tonic of the scale that has four sharps is ē, a perfect fifth higher than a, etc. (See Example 11.)

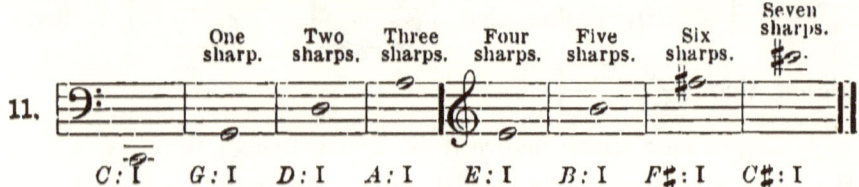

In the writing of seven other scales, flats are required. Play the scale beginning on f̄. The fourth tone is produced by playing the black key between ā and b̄. This tone is a half step lower than b̄, therefore b̄♭, and is written thus [image]. It must not be written ā♯, though the tone would be the same, for the third note from f̄, ā, must not be repeated.

The tonics of the scales with flats are to be found downwards from c̄, a perfect fifth apart.

The tonic of the scale that has one flat is f̄, a perfect fifth lower than c̄. The tonic of the scale that has two flats is b̄♭, a perfect fifth lower than f̄. The tonic of the scale that has three flats is ē♭, a perfect fifth lower than b̄♭, etc. (See Example 13.)

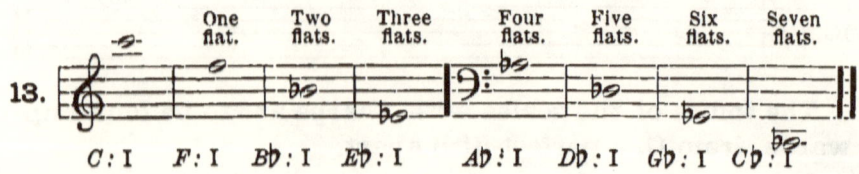

When a piece is written in the key of G, every F that occurs does not have a ♯ before it, but a ♯ is put at the beginning of the piece on the fifth line :   This means that every F is to be played sharp.

When a piece is written in the key of F, every B that occurs does not have a ♭ before it, but a flat is put at the beginning of the piece on the third line :   This means that every B that occurs is to be played flat.

It is the same with the other keys.

The sharps or flats of the key in which a composition is written are not indicated before the different notes, but are put at the beginning and effect the whole composition.   Sharps and flats thus indicated are called the **signature.**

Write out in your blank harmony book the scale of G, marking the whole and half steps, and the perfect and major intervals reckoned from G, in the same manner as you did in the key of C. Then write out the scale of D, and the perfect and major intervals reckoned from D.   Then the scales of A, E, B, F♯, C♯, and the perfect and major intervals from the tonic of each of these scales. Then write the scales that have flats and the perfect and major intervals from the tonic of each of these scales.*

***

Exercise in Ear Training.

Put the pupil at a distance from the piano, play the perfect intervals in the key of G as you did in the key of C, consecutively, then separately ; then play the major intervals in the same way

---

* The teacher may find it advisable for the pupil to wait till he has studied the twelve following chapters and written the relative minor scales of the scales with sharps, before he writes out the scales with flats and their relative minor scales.

until the pupil can recognize by ear any perfect or major interval from the tone G when it is struck separately. When this has been accomplished in the key of G, do the same in D, in E, etc., until the pupil gradually learns the perfect and major intervals from all the keynotes. This of course cannot be accomplished in a week or a month, but the exercise should be continued with other exercises. It might be taken up in the key in which the pupil is studying a composition, or in which he is practising a scale.

CHAPTER V.

The Primary Triads in Major.

A **chord** is three or more tones struck together. A chord of three tones is called a **triad**. We will first study a major triad. We can build a major triad on any tone. The tone we start from is the **root** of the triad; if we add to the root a **major third** and **perfect fifth** we have a **major triad.**

Major Triads.

14.

When this was explained to a little pupil, she was told to play a major triad and to take D as the root. "If D is the root, is the third the stem, and the fifth the leaves?" she asked. If we think of the tone from which we start as the root out of which the chord grows, this little pupil was not far wrong in wanting to have the third for the stem and the fifth for the leaves.

> Build a major triad on F.
> Build a major triad on D.
> Build a major triad on D♭.
> Build a major triad on E.
> Build a major triad on E♭, F♯, etc.

The triads built on the first, fourth, and fifth degrees of the major scale are **major triads.**

The triad built on the tonic is called the **tonic triad.**

The triad built on the dominant is called the **dominant triad.**

The triad built on the subdominant is called the **subdominant triad.**

The tonic, dominant, and subdominant triads are the **primary triads,** and together contain all the tones of the scale.

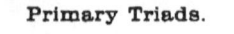

The tonic triad is designated by the Roman numeral I, written large.

The dominant triad is designated by the Roman numeral V, written large.

The subdominant triad is designated by the Roman numeral IV, written large.

The close relation of the primary triads to each other is shown in Example 15, *c.*

The root of the tonic triad is the fifth of the subdominant triad. The root of the dominant triad is the fifth of the tonic triad.

Notice that a triad can belong to more than one key.

A chord that has three tones can have three positions. When the root of the chord is the lowest tone, the chord is in the first position; when the third of the chord is the lowest tone, the chord is in the second position; when the fifth of the chord is the lowest tone, the chord is in the third position.

If in a chord you have two tones that are a fourth apart the upper one is the root:

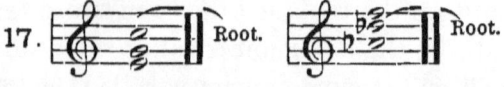

Open and Close Position of Triads.

The tones C, E, G form the chord of C. They form the chord of C whether they are played close together or far apart. If you should play C, ē, g̈, these three tones, although so far apart, would form the chord of C. When the tones of a chord are close together the chord is said to be in **close position**; when they are separated the chord is said to be in **open position**.

We shall learn more of close and open position in Chapter **XIX.**

Chords in Close and Open Position.

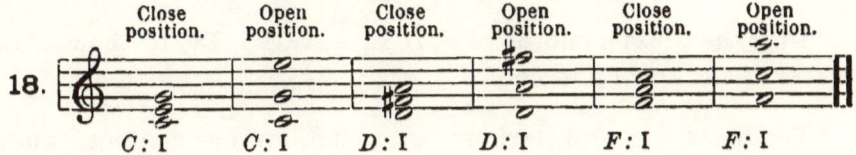

Broken Chords.

Often the tones that form a chord are not played together, the root of the chord can be played first, then the third, and then the fifth; thus the chord of C can be played:

The tones forming any chord can be struck in succession. A chord that has its tones struck in succession is called a **broken chord.**

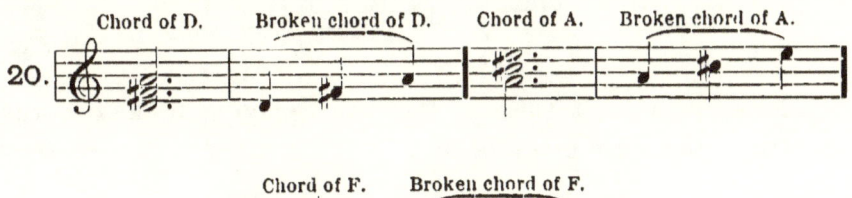

Play the broken chords of G, E, F♯, B, E♭, G♯.

Of course chords in their second and third position can also be played as broken chords.

Play the broken chords of **F, B, E, A, G, F♯, D♭**, in their first, second, and third positions.

The tones in a broken chord can also follow one another, thus :

After the root the fifth can be played, then the third, then the fifth again. This is a very common way of playing a broken chord. The second position of a chord thus broken would be :

The third position of a chord thus broken would be :

There are a great variety of ways of playing broken chords, several of these are given below :

Broken Triads.

C : I

C : I

C : I   C : I   D : I

D : I   D : I

D : I   D : I

In Ehmant's "Petite École Mélodique," Piece III, "The Chase" begins:

26.   C : I   C : I   C : I

In Example 26 the melody is played with the right hand, the chord that accompanies it with the left. You see that this chord is the tonic chord of C. Notice also that the tones occurring in the melody are tones belonging to the chord of C.

In Lebert & Starks' "Piano School" a popular melody begins:

27.

In Example 27 the chord that accompanies the melody is again the tonic chord of C, but this time the broken chord of C. Notice that the tones that occur in the melody belong to the chord of C.

In Reinecke's Collection of " Unsere Lieblinge," Piece III begins :

28.

The first three tones in the bass form the broken tonic chord of the key of G, which as you see is played four times.

You will find that all pieces of music end on a tonic chord, and that this last chord is generally on the accented beat of the measure. This tonic chord can be preceded by the dominant chord or by the subdominant chord. If it is preceded by the dominant chord the ending is called an authentic close or **authentic cadence.** Look at Piece II in the Schumann Album for the Young. It is a soldiers' march in the key of G. The last two measures are :

29.

The last chord is the tonic chord of the key of G on the accented beat of the measure; the chord that precedes it is the dominant chord of the key of G; the ending is therefore an authentic cadence.

When a piece ends on the tonic chord preceded by the subdominant chord, the ending is called a plagal close or a **plagal cadence.** In Harriet Jenks' Collection of Songs, the hymn, "The Careful Gardener," is in the key of C; the Amen of that hymn would be

30.

C: IV   I

The last chord is the tonic chord of the key of C on the accented beat of the measure; the chord that precedes it is the subdominant chord; the ending is therefore a plagal cadence.

We shall learn more of cadences in Chapters **XX, XXI,** and **XXII.**

Write out the fundamental chords in all the different keys, as shown on page 91, and practise playing them. Designate with Roman numerals the tonic, dominant and subdominant chords in the compositions upon which you are working.

Exercise in Ear Training.

Place the pupil where he cannot see the keyboard, play a tonic chord and after it the dominant or subdominant chord of the key. Ask the pupil to tell you which you have played.

CHAPTER VI.

Minor Intervals and Minor Triads.

We have learned that intervals are divided into perfect and major intervals and that from the perfect and major intervals all other intervals are formed. From major intervals minor intervals can be formed. A **minor interval** is formed by lowering the upper tone of a major interval a half step.

Minor means smaller. Therefore, when by lowering the upper tone of a major interval a smaller interval is formed, this interval is called a minor interval.

> Play a major second; change to a minor second.
> Play a major third; change to a minor third.
> Play a major sixth; change to a minor sixth.
> Play a major seventh; change to a minor seventh.
> Play a major ninth; change to a minor ninth.

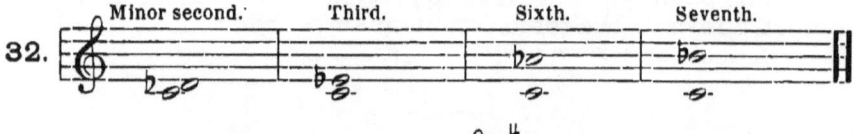

The major seventh from G is :

The minor seventh from G is : By taking the sharp away we have lowered the upper note a half step and do not of course need a flat.

When an interval is to be measured, its lowest tone must be thought of as the tonic of a major scale. If the upper tone of the interval belongs in the scale, it must be a perfect or a major interval; if it is a half step less than a major interval, it must be a minor interval.   If the interval 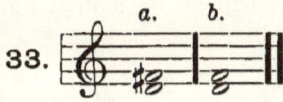 were to be measured,

d̄, the lowest tone, would have to be thought of as the tonic of the major scale of D.   F♯ is the third degree in the scale of D, f̄♮ would therefore be a minor (lesser) third.

"A minor interval is a major interval shortened," was a young pupil's definition of a minor interval.

A minor interval is a half step less than a major interval of the same primary name.   The **primary name** of an interval is the numerical name.

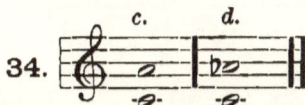

The primary name of the intervals in Example 33, *a* and *b*, is a third.   The third in Example 33, *a*, is a major third.   The third in Example 33, *b*, is a minor third.

The primary name of the intervals in Example 34, *c* and *d*, is a sixth.   The sixth in Example 34, *c*, is a major sixth.   The sixth in Example 34, *d*, is a minor sixth.

When you have to designate a difficult interval, it will be easier **first** to ascertain its primary name and then to think of the lowest tone as the tonic of a major scale.   You can easily ascertain the primary name of an interval by counting from the lowest to the highest note.   The lowest note of an interval is counted **one**.   The interval of a second is represented by two notes, the upper one of which is the second note from the first:

The upper note of the interval of a third must be the third note from the lowest note :

The upper note of the interval of a fourth must be the fourth note from the lowest note :

The upper note of the interval of a fifth must be the fifth note from the lowest note :

The intervals in Example 35, *a* and *b*, are enharmonic. The primary name of the interval in Example 35, *a*, is a second, because the upper tone is represented by the second note from the lowest note.

The primary name of the interval in Example 35, *b*, is a third, because the upper tone is represented by the third note from the lowest note.

Minor Triads.

A triad made up of a root, a minor third, and a perfect fifth is **a minor triad** :

How does a minor triad differ in its construction from a major triad?

The third in a minor triad differs from the third in a major triad; in a minor triad the third is minor, in a major triad the third is major.

You can easily distinguish a minor triad from a major triad, as a minor triad has a sad sound that a major triad does not have. A minor triad can be built on any tone.

> Build a minor triad on F.
> Build a minor triad on D.
> Build a minor triad on D♭.
> Build a minor triad on E.
> Build a minor triad on E♭, etc.

Broken Minor Triads.

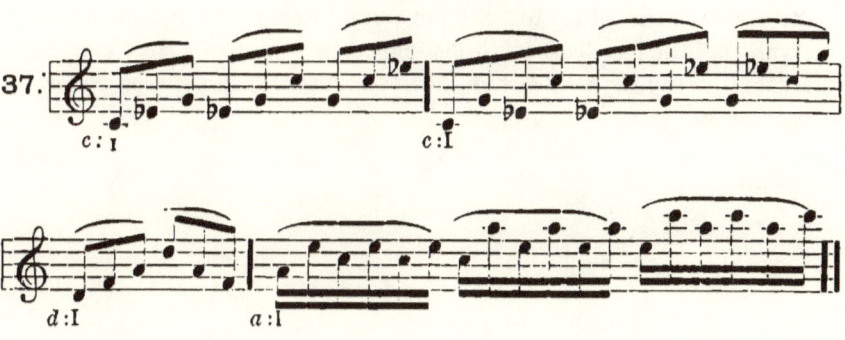

Write in your blank book on the page of C,* as shown on page 91, the minor intervals that can be formed from the major intervals, reckoned from the tonic of C major; on the page of G, the minor intervals that can be formed from the major intervals, reckoned from the tonic of G. On the pages of D, A, E, B, F♯, etc., the same.

---

* The page of C in the blank book is the page on which the scale of C is written, and on which are to be added intervals and chords belonging to the key of C. The other pages are designated in the same way.

Exercise in Ear Training.

Play the major and minor intervals from C in succession : Let the pupil distinguish between them. Then play the minor intervals from C separately. When the pupil has learnt to recognize these readily, play any perfect, major, or minor interval from C, and let the pupil try to name each one. Gradually treat the intervals from other keynotes in the same manner.

Play major and minor triads in succession, till the pupil can distinguish between them; then play major and minor triads separately, and let the pupil name each chord. Play also broken major and minor triads, and let the pupil distinguish between them.

REMARK. — Do not try to teach the pupil to recognize by ear the minor intervals until he has learned to distinguish readily the perfect and major intervals in many keys. Let him, however, distinguish between major and minor chords.

CHAPTER VII.

The Dominant Seventh Chord.

If to the dominant triad we add a minor seventh from the root, we have a chord of four tones . This chord is called the **dominant seventh chord.** It consists of a root, a major third, a perfect fifth, and a minor seventh, and is the most important chord of four tones. It is designated thus: V_7.

Strike the dominant chord of the key of G, add to it a minor seventh, and you will have:

38.

$$G : V_7$$

Build a dominant seventh chord on C, G, A, B, E, F♯, D♭, etc.

A chord that has four tones can have four positions:

First   Second   Third   Fourth   First   Second   Third   Fourth
position. position. position. position.   position. position. position. position.

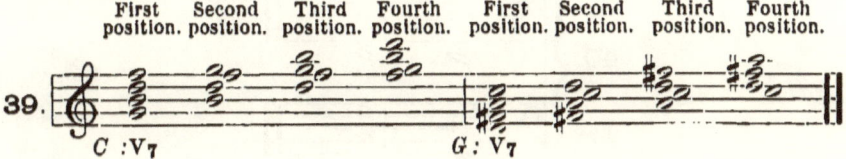

39.

$$C : V_7 \qquad\qquad G : V_7$$

When we have two tones in a chord, one step apart, the upper one is the root.

   Root.

If we had [image] in a chord, which would be the root?

If we had [image], which would be the root?

You have learned that a triad can belong to several keys. A given dominant seventh chord, however, can belong to but one major key. Each major key has a dominant seventh chord of its own, that no other major key can claim. Thus, wherever we find the chord  we know that we are in the key of C major, (or as we shall learn later in the minor key of the same name). For instance: this chord you hear played by some musician, who asks you in what major key he is playing. You can answer positively in the key of G major, because is the dominant seventh chord of the key of G major, and can belong to no other major key.

The dominant seventh chord is naturally followed by the tonic chord of the key to which it belongs; that is, the dominant seventh chord resolves to the tonic chord. The dominant seventh chord of the key of C resolves to the tonic chord of the key of C.

40.

$C : V_7 \qquad I$

The dominant seventh chord of the key of G resolves to the tonic chord of the key of G:

41.

$G : V_7 \qquad I$

The dominant seventh chord of the key of D resolves to the tonic chord of the key of D :

You can notice this in the music that you are studying. You will also notice that the fifth of the dominant seventh chord, the least important tone, is often left out.

Broken Dominant Seventh Chords.

A musical phrase is like a spoken sentence. They both express a thought ; one in tones, the other in words. For instance :

Notice what a complete musical phrase you have given in these three chords. The tonic chord begins the phrase, the dominant seventh chord adds something of more interest, and then the tonic chord brings the phrase to a satisfactory end.

The chords of many little pieces and studies consist entirely of the tonic and dominant seventh chords.   In the first study from Germer's collection of Czerny's studies, given below, the chords throughout are either the tonic or the dominant seventh chord.

Study.

45.

Also in the three following studies of this collection, the only chords used are the tonic and dominant seventh chords.

In the "Zigeunertanz" by Weber, Piece 26, from Reinecke's collection of "Unsere Lieblinge" (Breitkopf & Härtel Ed.), given below, the only chords used are the tonic and dominant seventh chords.

Play this little piece and notice the construction of the chords.

Zigeunertanz.   WEBER.

46.

You noticed that in Chapter V, in Examples 26, 27, and 28, the tones that occurred in the melody were also found in the accompanying harmony.

Look at the first measure in Example 46. The notes in the melody that are marked thus : ✕ are notes that belong to the chord of C, whereas the notes marked thus : – are discordant with the chord of C.

Notes that the melody touches in passing from a note to another of a chord are called **passing notes**. Therefore the second, fourth, and eighth notes in Example 46 in the first measure are called passing notes.

A note that the melody touches, between a note of a chord and the repetition of the same note is also called a passing note. This passing note can be the next note in the scale to the melody note, either above or below. Such a passing note is the sixth note in the first measure in Example 46.

Play the Czerny Study, Example 45. Distinguish between the notes that belong to the different chords, and the passing

notes. The notes belonging to the chords are marked thus: ×,
the passing notes thus: – .

You will also find passing notes in accompaniments. It is impossible here to go further into the subject of passing notes. As
you advance in the study of music, light will be thrown upon
many things which now seem incomprehensible.

**Write the dominant seventh chords in all the major keys, as
shown on page 91, in four positions, and practise playing them.**
**Designate the dominant seventh chords in the compositions
you are studying.**

When a piece ends on a tonic chord preceded by a dominant
seventh chord, the ending is a perfect close or a **perfect cadence.**

The last two measures of Haydn's Austrian Hymn are:

47.

$G : V_7$ $G : I$

The last chord is the tonic chord of the key of G on the accented beat of the measure; it is preceded by the dominant
seventh chord of the key of G, the ending is therefore a perfect
cadence.

Exercise in Ear Training.

Let the pupil distinguish between a dominant triad and a
dominant seventh chord at a distance from the piano and learn
to recognize a dominant seventh chord when it is struck separately. Play also broken dominant triads and broken dominant
seventh chords, and let the pupil distinguish between them.

CHAPTER VIII.

Diminished Intervals.

From major intervals smaller intervals can be formed, which are called minor intervals.

From perfect intervals smaller intervals can be formed which are called **diminished intervals** (that is intervals made smaller). A diminished interval is formed from a perfect interval by lowering the upper tone a half step, or by raising the lower tone a half step.

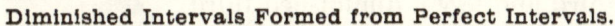

Diminished Intervals Formed from Perfect Intervals.

Sometimes in the progress of a melody a diminished prime is found :

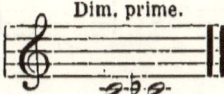

It is never used in building up chords. It is formed by lowering one or the other tone of the perfect prime a half step.

From minor intervals smaller intervals can be formed, which are also called **diminished intervals.** A diminished interval is formed from a minor interval by lowering the upper tone a half step, or by raising the lower tone a half step.

Diminished Intervals Formed from Minor Intervals.

Diminished seconds are not intervals but are enharmonic tones

If the interval [staff] were to be measured, b̄ would have to be thought of as the tonic of the major scale of B. F♯ is the fifth degree of the scale of B, f̄♯ would therefore be a diminished fifth.

If the interval [staff] were to be measured, the lowest tone, c̄, would have to be thought of as the tonic of a major scale. E♮ is the third of the scale of C, E♭ therefore would be a minor third and ē♭♭ a diminished third.

A diminished interval is a whole step less than a major interval of the same primary name, and a half step less than a perfect interval of the same primary name.

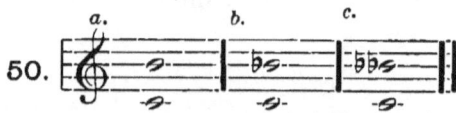

The primary name of the intervals in Example 50, *a*, *b*, and *c*, is a seventh. The seventh in Example *a* is a major seventh. The seventh in Example *b* is a minor seventh. The seventh in Example *c* is a diminished seventh.

A story is told of Teresa Carrẽno, the now famous pianist, picking out a diminished seventh when she was only three years old. The child had been tucked up in her little crib for the night, but she could not sleep. A famous dance of that time, a Varsovienne that her older sister had been practising the day before, was running through her little brain. She climbed out of her crib and found her way to the piano, and began to pick out the notes. She succeeded well till she came to a queer interval for which she had to fumble and hunt. Sen. Carrẽno, Teresa's father, hearing uncertain touches on the piano, thought it was Teresa's older sister practising, and came in to tell her the right notes. What was his surprise to find little Teresa on tip toe at

the piano, her shoulders on a level with the keyboard, and just
striking the interval that had evaded her at first ; it was a diminished seventh.　There are many Varsoviennes ; there is one of
that time which has this diminished seventh in it , and
very likely this may have been the diminished seventh little
Teresa Carreño picked out.

When you have written the intervals from the tonic of all the
keys that have sharps as shown in the Table on page 91, and are
ready to write the intervals from the tonic of the keys that have
flats, you must study the paragraphs below.

Form the intervals from F, the tonic of the key that has one
flat, as you have formed them.

Form the diminished intervals from Bb, Eb, Ab, Db, Gb, Cb,
the tonics of the keys that have two, three, four, five, six, and
seven flats, in one way only, by raising the lower note a half step.
If you formed the diminished intervals by lowering the upper
note you would have to use a great many flats.　Therefore, in a
key with a signature of flats, diminished intervals are usually
formed by raising the lower note a half step.　For instance, the
major third from gb is , the minor third is ,
the diminished third can be formed only by raising the lower
note a half step, thus : .　You could not form it by
lowering the upper note a half step, for then you would have to
use a triple flat which is never written in music.

Write out the diminished intervals that can be formed from
the perfect and major intervals of the key of C (reckoned from
C,) as shown on page 91, those formed from the perfect and
major intervals reckoned from G on the page of G, etc., through
all the different major keys.

Exercise in Ear Training.

Let the pupil distinguish at a distance from the piano the perfect intervals from the diminished intervals. Play a perfect fourth or fifth followed by a diminished fourth or fifth.

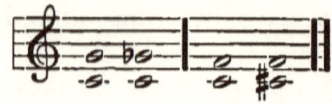

Let him tell you whether you have raised the lower tone or lowered the upper tone in forming a diminished fourth or fifth. Let him distinguish the minor from the diminished intervals. Play a major, minor, or diminished third, tell the pupil it is a third, and let him tell you what kind of a third it is.

CHAPTER IX.

Augmented Intervals.

We have learned how smaller intervals are formed from perfect and major intervals. We are now to study how augmented intervals (that is intervals made larger) are formed. Both from perfect and major intervals **augmented intervals** can be formed by raising the upper tone a half step.

An augmented prime is formed from a perfect prime by raising one or the other tone a half step.

Augmented Intervals Formed from Perfect Intervals.

51.

Augmented Intervals Formed from Major Intervals.

52.

Augmented sevenths never occur.

If the interval 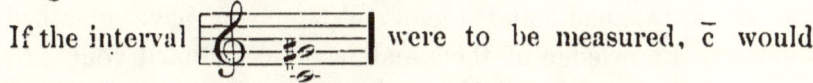 were to be measured, $\bar{c}$ would have to be thought of as the tonic of the major scale of C. G is the fifth degree of the scale of C, $\bar{g}\sharp$ would therefore be an augmented fifth.

An augmented interval is a half step larger than a major or a perfect interval of the same primary name.

53.

The primary name of the intervals in Example 53, *a*, *b*, and *c*, is a second. The second in Example 53, *a*, is a major second. The second in Example 53, *b*, is an augmented second. The second in Example 53, *c*, is a minor second.

Summary of Intervals.

The intervals of the major scale reckoned from the tonic are **perfect** or **major**. From **perfect** intervals diminished and augmented intervals can be formed. From **major** intervals minor and augmented intervals can be formed. From **minor** intervals diminished intervals can be formed.

A **minor** interval is smaller by a half step than a major interval of the same primary name. A **diminished** interval is smaller by a half step than a perfect or a minor interval of the same primary name. A **diminished** interval is smaller by a whole step than a major interval of the same primary name. An **augmented** interval is larger by a half step than a perfect or a major interval of the same primary name.

You see how clear and simple the intervals are, and how essential it is to understand them. When you have obtained a thorough knowledge of them and have accustomed your ear to recognize them, you will have taken a long step on the road to becoming a good musician.

Dr. S. Jadassohn, professor at the Royal Conservatory of Music at Leipzig says: "The pupil should so accustom his ear to the pitch of the different intervals, that he can always recognize them."

Write out in your blank harmony book the augmented intervals; write the augmented intervals that are formed from the perfect and major intervals of the key of C, (reckoned from the tonic,) on the page of C, as shown on page 91; the augmented intervals that are formed from the perfect and major intervals reckoned from G, on the page of G, etc.

Exercise in Ear Training.

Let the pupil (not seeing the keyboard) distinguish between the augmented and perfect intervals, the major and augmented. Play a perfect fifth followed by an augmented fifth, thus:

. Let the pupil tell you which is perfect and which augmented. Then play an augmented, perfect or diminished fifth. Tell the pupil it is a fifth, and let him tell you which kind of a fifth it is, etc.

CHAPTER X.

The Secondary Triads in Major.

The triads built on the first, fourth, and fifth tones of the scale are the primary triads of the key; the triads built on the remaining tones of the scale, on the second, third, sixth, and seventh tones, are the **secondary triads**:

Secondary Triads in Major.

The triads built on the second, third, and sixth tones of the major scale are minor triads.

The triad built on the seventh tone of the scale of C is made up of its root, a minor third, and a diminished fifth.

A triad made up of **its root, a minor third, and a diminished fifth is a diminished triad.**

Build diminished triads on C, F, E, D, B, B♭, etc.

The triad built on the seventh tone of the major scale is a diminished triad.

We have studied three different kinds of triads: major, minor and diminished triads.

A **major triad** is made up of its root, a major third, and a perfect fifth.

A **minor triad** is made up of its root, a minor third, and a perfect fifth.

A **diminished triad** is made up of its root, a minor third, and a diminished fifth.

The Roman numerals, as we have said before, designating major triads are written large. The chords built on the tonic, dominant and subdominant of the major scale are designated thus : I, V, IV.

The Roman numerals designating minor triads are written small, to distinguish them from major triads. The triads built on the second, third, and sixth tones of the major scale are designated thus : ii, iii. vi. The Roman numerals designating diminished triads are written small with an o after them, to distinguish them from minor triads. The triad built on the seventh tone of the major scale is designated thus vii°.

Relative Keys.

Some keys have many tones in common, others have few tones in common, and some keys have no tones in common.

The key of C and the key of G have all but one tone in common, the tone of F♯. The key of G and the key of D have all but one tone in common, the tone of C♯. Keys that have many tones in common are called **relative keys.** Keys that have many tones in common have of course many triads formed of their tones, in common. The key of C and the key of G have four of their triads in common.

The triads common to the two keys are marked with a ✕. The major triads of C and G are common to the two keys ; the minor triads of *e* and *a* are common to the two keys.

The close relationship of one key to another must never be forgotten.

Write the secondary triads that are built on the different tones of the major scale, in all major keys as shown on page 91.

Exercise in Ear Training.

Place the pupil at a distance from the piano and play the different triads — major, minor, and diminished — until he can readily recognize them whether played in succession or separately. Let him also distinguish between broken major, minor, and diminished triads.

CHAPTER XI.

Consonances and Dissonances : Dependent and Independent Chords.

The perfect and major intervals and the intervals formed from these, the minor, diminished, and augmented intervals, are classed as **consonances** or **dissonances**. It is not difficult to distinguish the consonances from the dissonances. The consonances are the harmonious and smoother intervals ; the dissonances are the less harmonious and rougher intervals.

Play the normal intervals of the major scale.

Normal Intervals.

56.

The prime, fourth, fifth, and octave, and the third and sixth are harmonious intervals, therefore consonances ; the second and seventh are inharmonious intervals, therefore dissonances.

Consonances are divided into **perfect** and **imperfect consonances.** The perfect consonances are the perfect intervals.

Perfect Consonances.

57.

The imperfect consonances are the major and minor third and the major and minor sixth :

Imperfect Consonances.

58.

The perfect prime and perfect octave are the smoothest consonances.

The **dissonances** are the major and minor second, the major and minor seventh, and all augmented and diminished intervals.

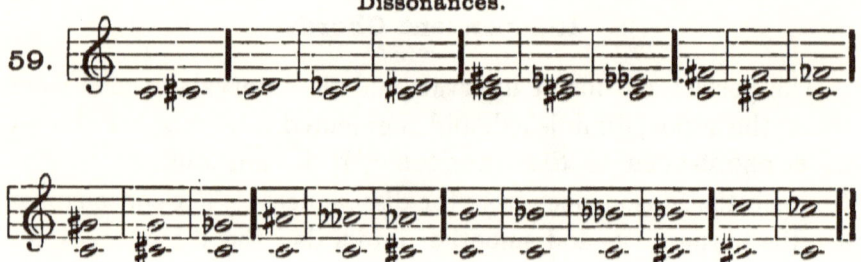

Dissonances.

59.

The minor seventh is the smoothest of all dissonances and the minor second the roughest of all dissonances.

Dissonances to satisfy the ear have to be followed by other intervals, that is, they have to be resolved to consonances. When you hear certain words, for instance "whichever," "but," "and," you know that other words will follow; dissonances are like these words. When you hear dissonances, for instance, 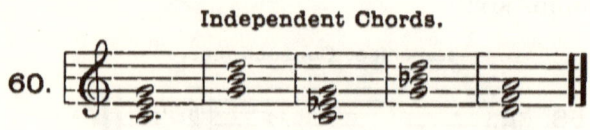 you know that other intervals will follow.

Dependent and Independent Chords.

A chord composed entirely of consonant intervals is an **independent chord.** It satisfies the ear so completely that it does not have to be resolved.

Independent Chords.

60.

A chord that contains a dissonant interval is a **dependent chord.**

Dependent Chords.

61.

Dependent chords are like dissonances, they are not complete in themselves. A dependent chord to satisfy the ear must be followed by another chord, that is, it must be resolved to an independent chord.

The major and minor triads are the only independent chords. All other chords are dependent chords and have to be resolved to independent chords. Sometimes several dependent chords occur in succession. When this happens the last one resolves to an independent chord.

The last chord of a composition must always be one of the independent chords, a major or a minor chord. The two dependent chords that you have already studied are the dominant seventh chord and the diminished triad.

Play   and   . Neither of these chords could possibly be the final chord of a composition.

Here are the last two measures of Schumann's " Happy Farmer ":

F:V$_7$ F:I

You see how impossible it would be to stop on the chord that precedes the last. It is only when the last chord has been played that you have a sense of repose.   If the piece ended with the chord preceding the last, your ear would not be satisfied. Notice also that this dependent chord with its dissonant seventh brings out by its very dissonance the sense of rest in the final chord.

Exercise in Ear Training.

Play consonant and dissonant intervals; let the pupil distinguish between them.   Play dependent and independent chords; let the pupil try to tell which you have played.   The pupil must be where he cannot see the keyboard.

CHAPTER XII.

Inversion of Intervals.

is a perfect fifth.   If the $\bar{\bar{g}}$ is played an octave lower, that is, if the interval is **inverted** (turned over), it forms a perfect fourth :   .

is a perfect fourth ; when it is inverted it forms a perfect fifth :   .

is a perfect prime ; when it is inverted it forms a perfect octave :   .

A precious stone carefully polished on all sides is put into your hand ; you are told that it is perfect.   You turn it upside down and find the bottom perfect ; every side of the stone is perfect.   Thus it is with intervals in music ; the ones that are called perfect remain perfect when they are turned upside down, that is, when they are inverted.

Major intervals inverted form minor intervals, minor intervals inverted form major intervals, diminished intervals inverted form augmented intervals, augmented intervals inverted form diminished intervals.

Perfect intervals are the only intervals that remain the same when they are inverted ; all other intervals are changed.

Perfect Intervals Inverted Remain Perfect.

| Perfect prime. | Perfect octave. | Perfect fourth. | Perfect fifth. | Perfect fiftn. | Perfect fourth. | Perfect octave. | Perfect prime. |

63.

Major Intervals Inverted Become Minor Intervals.

Minor Intervals Inverted Become Major Intervals.

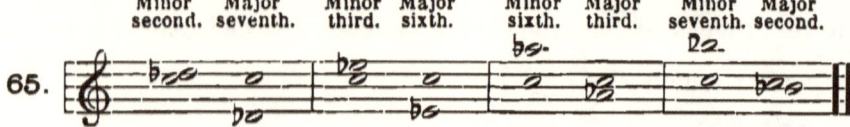

Diminished Intervals Inverted Become Augmented Intervals.

Augmented Intervals Inverted Become Diminished Intervals.

Notice that a second when it is inverted becomes a seventh, together making the number nine.

Notice that a third when it is inverted becomes a sixth, together making the number nine.

Notice that a fourth when it is inverted becomes a fifth, together making the number nine.

Notice that a fifth when it is inverted becomes a fourth, together making the number nine.

Notice that a sixth when it is inverted becomes a third, together making the number nine.

Notice that a seventh when it is inverted becomes a second together making the number nine.

Notice that an eighth when it is inverted becomes a prime, together making the number nine.

CHAPTER XIII.

The Harmonic Minor Scale.

Each major scale has a closely related scale, which is formed out of its tones. This scale is called a **minor scale**. It begins on the sixth tone of the major scale, to which it is related. C major is therefore related to *a* minor.

68.

The scale of *a* minor, as shown in Example 68, *b*, has the same tones as its relative major scale, C major. This was the original minor scale. Musicians, however, were not satisfied with it. A scale must have a leading tone ; the seventh tone of this scale was a whole step from the tonic above, and for that reason could not be a true leading tone. The seventh tone was therefore raised a half step in order to make it a true and satisfactory leading tone.

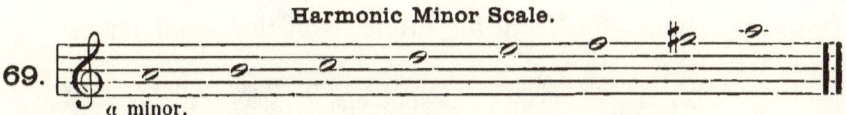

69.

The scale as shown in Example 69, is our harmonic minor scale ; it has the same tones as its relative major scale with the exception of the seventh tone.

Find the tonic of the minor scale related to G major.
Find the tonic of the minor scale related to D major.
Find the tonic of the minor scale related to F♯ major.
Find the tonic of the minor scale related to B major, etc.

The tones of the minor scale do not follow one another in the same order as the tones of the major scale.

From the first degree to the second degree is a whole step.

From the second degree to the third degree is a half step.

From the third degree to the fourth degree is a whole step.

From the fourth degree to the fifth degree is a whole step.

From the fifth degree to the sixth degree is a half step.

From the sixth degree to the seventh degree is a step and a half.

From the seventh degree to the eighth degree (octave of the tonic) is a half step.

70.

The half steps are between the second and third, the fifth and sixth, the seventh and eighth degrees; between the sixth and seventh degrees there is a step and a half, and between the other degrees a whole step.

Form the harmonic minor scale from e, b♭, a, c, d, etc.

We must see which intervals of the minor scale, reckoned from the tonic, differ from the intervals of the major scale.

71.

a minor.

What is the interval from the first to the second tone? *A major second.*

What is the interval from the first to the third tone? *A minor third.*

What is the interval from the first to the fourth tone? *A perfect fourth.*

What is the interval from the first to the fifth tone? *A perfect fifth.*

What is the interval from the first to the sixth tone? *A minor sixth.*

What is the interval from the first to the seventh tone? *A major seventh.*

What is the interval from the first to the eighth tone? *A perfect octave.*

What two intervals are not the same as the intervals of the major scale? *The third and the sixth, which are minor in the minor scale.*

For this reason the *minor* scale has received the name *minor.*

The tones that form a major scale constitute a major key or a major family of tones.

The tones C, D, E, F, G, A, B constitute the key of C major, whether they are struck together as chords or follow one another in an endless variety of ways. The relationship of the tones remains the same, as the relationship of the members of a family is the same whether they are arranged in regular order or not. When the tones are played in successive order, they form the major scale.

It is thus in minor keys or minor families of tones. The tones that form a minor scale constitute a minor key.

There are **two modes** in music, the major and the minor mode. These may not inappropriately be spoken of as races.

All the major families of tones, the major keys, belong to the major race of tones — the major mode.

All the minor families of tones, the minor keys, belong to the minor race of tones — the minor mode.

Learn to say the order of succession of the harmonic minor scale, as you did of the major scale, forward and backward. Write the relative minor scale of each major scale, and the intervals reckoned from the tonic of each, as shown on page 92.

Exercise in Ear Training.

Play major and minor scales. Let the pupil distinguish, not seeing the keyboard, a minor from a major scale.

CHAPTER XIV.

The Primary Triads in Minor.

The first, fourth, and fifth tones of the minor, as well as of the major scale, are called the **tonic**, the **dominant**, and the **subdominant**.

The triads built on the tonic, dominant, and subdominant are called the tonic, dominant, and subdominant triads. They are the **primary triads** of a minor as well as of a major key.

The tonic triad of a minor key is minor.

The dominant triad of a minor key is major.

The subdominant triad of a minor key is minor.

A major key is designated by a capital letter. A minor key by a small letter.

Primary Triads in Minor.

Which of the primary triads of a minor key differ in their construction from the primary triads of a major key? *The tonic and subdominant triads which are minor in a minor key.*

Which primary triad is the same as in a major key? *The dominant triad which is major in both modes.*

The dominant seventh chord in a minor key has the same construction as the dominant seventh chord in a major key.

It is made up of its root, a major third, a perfect fifth, and a minor seventh.

In the key of A major and *a* minor the dominant seventh chord is :

It is in the key of *a* minor if it resolves to the tonic chord of
a minor; it is in the key of A major if it resolves to the tonic
chord of A major.

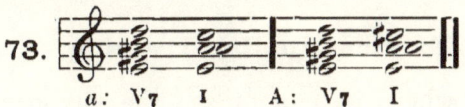

The dominant seventh chords in Example 74, *a* and, *b* are the
same:

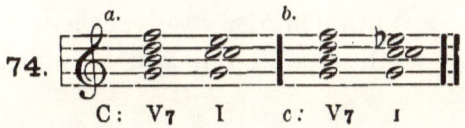

The dominant seventh chord in Example 74, *a*, belongs to the
key of C major, as it resolves to the tonic triad of C major. The
dominant seventh chord in Example 74, *b*, belongs to the key of
c minor, as it resolves to the tonic triad of *c* minor.

A dominant seventh chord can belong to a major or a minor
key of the same name.

Given below is the first phrase of a little piece by Theodore
Oesten, from Op. 167, Book I. The phrase is in the key of *a*
minor; the dominant seventh chord in the third measure resolves
to the tonic chord of *a* minor in the fourth measure.

Write the primary triads and the dominant seventh chords, as shown on page 92, in all the minor keys, and practise playing them.

Exercise in Ear Training.

Put the pupil where he cannot see the keyboard. Play the tonic chord of a minor key ; after it the dominant, subdominant, or dominant seventh chord of the key. Let the pupil tell you which you have played.

Play dominant seventh chords, resolve them to major or minor chords, and let the pupil tell you to which you have resolved them.

Play also broken dominant seventh chords, resolve them to broken major or minor chords, and let the pupil tell you to which you have resolved them.

CHAPTER XV.

The Secondary Triads in Minor.

The **secondary triads** of a minor key are built on the second, third, sixth, and seventh degrees of the minor scale. They are built on the same degrees of the scale as the secondary triads of a major key.

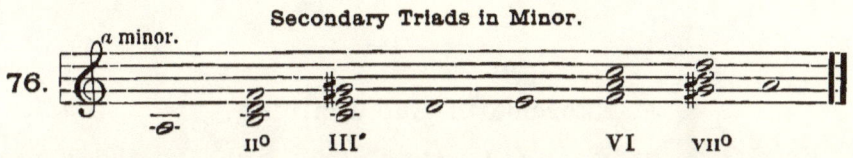

Secondary Triads in Minor.

The triads built on the second and seventh degrees of the minor scale are diminished triads. The triad built on the sixth degree of the minor scale is a major triad.

The triad built on the third degree of the minor scale we have not studied, as yet; it is an augmented triad.

An **augmented triad** is made up of its root, a major third, and an augmented fifth.

The triad built on the third degree of the scale of *a* minor is:

From $\bar{c}$ to $\bar{g}\sharp$ is an augmented fifth.

The triad built on the third degree of the scale of *g* minor is:

From b♭ to $\bar{f}\sharp$ is an augmented fifth.

The interval from the root to the fifth of the augmented triad is an augmented fifth; therefore the triad is called an augmented triad. Build augmented triads on D, B, A, F, C♯, etc.

A Roman numeral designating an augmented triad is written large with an accent after it. The triad built on the third tone of the minor scale is designated thus III′.

Write out the triads built on the different tones of the minor scale in all the minor keys, as shown on page 92.

- - - - - - -

Exercise in Ear Training.

Let the pupil distinguish, without seeing the keyboard, between major, minor, diminished, and augmented triads, and learn to recognize them when they are played separately.

Play also broken major, minor, diminished, and augmented triads, and let the pupil distinguish between them.

CHAPTER XVI.

The Melodic Minor Scale.

Between the sixth and seventh tones of the minor scale there is an augmented second.   In *a* minor:

The interval of an augmented second is very difficult for singers to intonate; therefore it has to be avoided in vocal music. This is usually done by raising the sixth tone a half step when ascending the scale, and lowering the seventh tone a half step when descending the scale.   The harmonic minor scale thus changed is called the **melodic minor scale.**

Harmonic Minor Scale of a.

77.

Melodic Minor Scale of a.

Harmonic Minor Scale of e.

Melodic Minor Scale of e.

The harmonic minor scale is the important one in harmony, for from its tones the chords of a minor key are built.

Build a melodic minor scale on d, b, e, g, a, c, etc.

Learn to say the order of succession of the melodic minor scale as you did of the major scale, forward and backward. Write the melodic minor scale, from the tonic of each harmonic minor scale, as shown on page 92.

Exercise in Ear Training.

Play harmonic and melodic minor scales; let the pupil distinguish between them and learn to recognize each when it is played separately.

CHAPTER XVII.

Signature of Major and Minor Keys.

A **major key** and its **relative minor key** have the same **signature.** The beginning and end of a piece show in which key it is written.

For example, a piece with the signature of one sharp is in the key of G major or *e* minor.

A piece begins with tones or a chord belonging to the key in which it is said to be written, usually the tonic chord, and ends on the tonic chord of the same key.

The key of C major and its relative minor key, *a* minor, have no signature.

I. " Melodie," in Schumann's " Album for the Young," has no signature ; it is therefore in the key of C major or *a* minor.

Before we can tell if it is in C major or *a* minor we must see how the piece begins and ends.

The first measure is :

The last measure is :

The first measure begins with tones that form the tonic chord of C major; the last measure ends with tones that form the tonic chord of C major, therefore the piece is in the key of C major.

Piece 6, in Schumann's " Album for the Young," has no signature. It is therefore in the key of C major or *a* minor; the beginning and end of the piece will show in which key it is written.

The first measure is:

The last measure is:

The piece is clearly in the key of *a* minor; the first tone is the tonic of *a* minor; the first chord is the tonic chord of *a* minor, and the piece ends on the tonic chord of *a* minor.

The keys of G major and *e* minor have the signature of one sharp:

D major and *b* minor have the signature of two sharps:

A major and *f♯* minor have the signature of three sharps :

E major and *c♯* minor have the signature of four sharps :

B major and *g♯* minor have the signature of five sharps :

F♯ major and *d♯* minor have the signature of six sharps :

C♯ major and *a♯* minor have the signature of seven sharps :

F major and *d* minor have the signature of one flat :

Piece 10, in Schumann's "Album for the Young," has the signature of one flat; therefore it is in the key of F major or *d* minor.

The first measure is :

The last measure is :

The first tones that are played by the left hand belong to the tonic chord of F major; the first chord that is played by the right hand is the tonic chord of F major, and the piece ends on the tonic chord of F major, therefore it is in the key of F major.

Piece 9, in Schumann's "Album for the Young," has the signature of one flat; it is therefore in the key of F major or *d* minor.

The first measure is:

84.

The last measure is:

85.

The tones of the first half of the first measure form the tonic chord of *d* minor, and the piece ends on the tonic chord of *d* minor; therefore it is in the key of *d* minor.

The keys of B♭ major and *g* minor have the signature of two flats:

E♭ major and *c* minor have the signature of three flats:

A♭ major and *f* minor have the signature of four flats:

D♭ major and *b♭* minor have the signature of five flats:

G♭ major and *e♭* minor have the signature of six flats:

C♭ major and *a♭* minor have the signature of seven flats:

Exercise in Ear Training.

Play the beginning and end of various pieces to the pupil; tell him the signature of each, and let him tell you in what key each is written. The pupil must be where he cannot see the keyboard.

CHAPTER XVIII.

Modulation.

A musical composition begins and ends in the same key, but throughout the composition many foreign keys may be introduced.

Modulation means passing out of one key into another key.

If a piece begins in the key of C and then changes to the key of G, this changing from one key to another key is modulating from one key to another key. Modulation usually takes place between relative keys. A very common modulation is to the key of the dominant, that is, to the key the tonic of which is the dominant of the key from which the modulation is made:

From the key of C to the key of G.

From the key of D to the key of A.

From the key of E to the key of B, etc.

Another common modulation is from a major key to its relative minor key:

From C major to *a* minor.

From B major to *g*♯ minor.

From D major to *b* minor, etc.

In the "Schumann Album," Op. 68, the first piece, "Melodie," in C major, has in the fourth measure a modulation to the dominant key, that is to the key of G major.

86.   G: V₇   I

On the second beat of the measure we have the dominant

seventh chord of the key of G, and on the third beat the tonic chord of the key of G major.

We have learned that a given dominant seventh chord can belong only to a major key or to a minor key of the same name. You know that a modulation has taken place to the key of G major when you see the dominant seventh chord followed by the tonic chord of G major.

In the second piece of the Schumann Album, in the "Soldier's March," in G major, there is a modulation in the seventh measure to the dominant key of D major:

87.

D: vii°   D: I   D: V₇   D: I

The first chord in the seventh measure is built on the leading tone of the key of D major. The second chord in the seventh measure is the tonic chord of D major. The first chord in the eighth measure is the dominant seventh chord of the key of D major, and the second chord in the eighth measure is the tonic chord of D major.

In the Beethoven "Sonatina," in G major, in the fifth measure, there is a modulation to the key of C major:

88.

C: V₇   I

The bass of the last half of the fifth measure is the broken dominant seventh chord of the key of C major. The bass of the first half of the sixth measure is the broken tonic chord of the key of C major. In the last half of the sixth measure we are again in the key of G major.

Exercise in Ear Training.

Play simple pieces to the pupil; tell him when a modulation takes place, till gradually he will be able to recognize a change of key; let him try to tell you if the modulation has taken place to a major or a minor key, and when the piece returns to the original key.

CHAPTER XIX.

Doubling the tones of a Triad; Open and Close Position of Chords.

A triad is a chord of three tones; but often a triad needs **four parts,** in which case one of its tones is **doubled.**

The root of a triad is commonly doubled:

The fifth of a triad can be doubled, but not as often as the root:

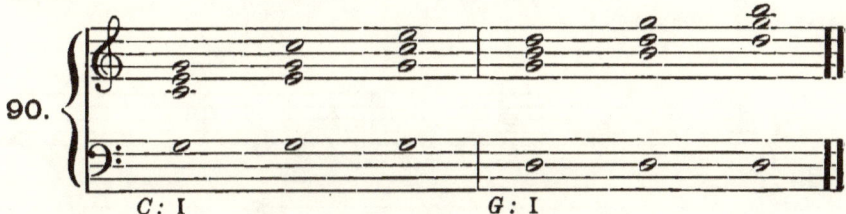

The third of a triad is least often doubled:

When one of the tones of a triad has been doubled, the chord may still be called a triad. There are still three different tones, though one of them has been doubled.

You must have distinguished in a church quartet four different voices.

The highest voice is the **soprano**.

The next highest voice is the **alto**.

The voice below that is the **tenor**.

The lowest voice is the **bass**.

Thus in chords we will think of the parts as soprano, alto, tenor, and bass:

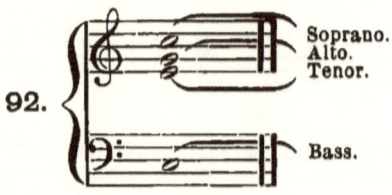

A great deal of music is written in four parts. These may easily be distinguished in Schumann's "Choral." Here are the first four measures:

Here the last note in the last measure has two stems; this means that it belongs to two parts. If this Choral were sung the soprano and alto would both sing d̄.

Open and Close Position of Chords.

A chord is in **close position** when the three upper parts are within the compass of an octave, even though the bass is much lower.

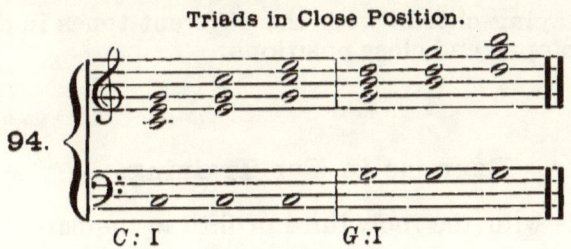

Triads in Close Position.

94.   *C : I*   *G : I*

A chord is in **open position** when the three upper parts are spread out beyond the compass of an octave.

Triads in Open Position.

95.   *C : I*   *G : I*

The triad in Example 95, *a*, is in open position; the three upper parts are spread out beyond the compass of an octave.

For the same reason the triads in Example 95, *b*, *c*, *d*, *e*, and *f*, are in open position.

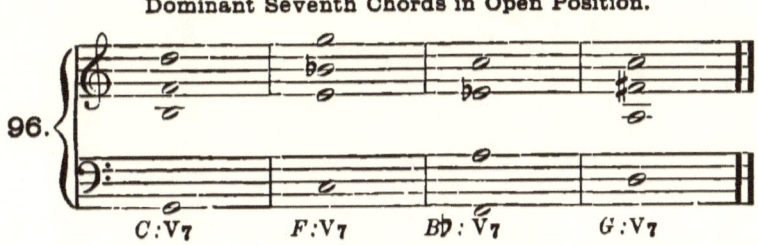

Dominant Seventh Chords in Open Position.

96. $C:V_7$ $F:V_7$ $B\flat:V_7$ $G:V_7$

Practise playing chords with the different tones in the bass, and chords in open and close positions.

Exercise in Ear Training.

Play chords with the root, third or fifth in the bass. Let the pupil try to distinguish which interval is in the bass. Play chords in open and close positions. Let the pupil distinguish between them. The pupil must be where he cannot see the keyboard.

CHAPTER XX.

The Authentic Cadence.

A cadence is the close of a strain or of a piece of music. There are three kinds of cadences : the authentic, the perfect, and the plagal cadence.

The last chord of a cadence is the tonic chord, which generally enters on an accented part of the measure. When the tonic chord is preceded by the dominant chord the close is called an **authentic cadence.**

Authentic Cadences.

79.

C :V   I   G :V   I   F :V   I

That you may be able to play cadences correctly in all the different keys, you are now to learn the first rules about connecting chords.

a. Good.   *b.* Not good.   *c.* Not good.

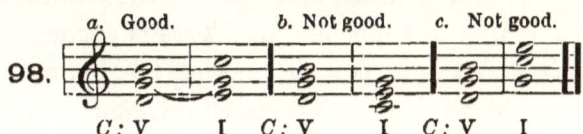

98.

C : V   I   C : V   I   C : V   I

In Example 98, *a*, the dominant chord is followed by the tonic chord in such a way that the chords sound connected, whereas in Example 98, *b* and *c*, the chords sound disconnected. In order that chords may follow one another smoothly certain rules have been established :

When in two successive chords there is a common tone it must remain in the **same part** in both chords, and the other tones must be led to those of the next chord which lie nearest to them :

Both chords in Example 99 having $\bar{g}$ in them, $\bar{g}$ is the common tone. The alto has $\bar{g}$ in the dominant chord ; therefore the alto must keep $\bar{g}$ in the tonic chord :

What tone is common in the two chords in Example 100 ? *The common tone is* $\bar{e}$. The alto has $\bar{e}$ in the dominant chord ; therefore the alto must keep $\bar{e}$ in the tonic chord.

In Example 98, *a*, the common tone $\bar{g}$ has been kept in the alto part ; that is, in the same part in both chords, and this is correct. In Example 98, *b*, the common tone $\bar{g}$ has not been kept in the same part in both chords ; it is in the alto part in the dominant chord, and in the soprano part in the tonic chord, which is incorrect.

In Example 98, *a*, $\bar{d}$ is in the tenor part in the dominant chord, and is led to $\bar{e}$ in the tonic chord. This is correct. In Example 98, *c*, the tenor is at fault in making the jump from $\bar{d}$ in the dominant chord to $\bar{g}$ in the tonic chord, and in not moving to the nearest tone.

If in two successive chords the first has the leading tone and the second the tonic, the leading tone is led a half step upward to the tonic :

The **dominant** tone, root of the dominant chord, in the bass
of an authentic cadence is led a skip of a fourth upward or a fifth
downward to the **tonic** in the following chord:

102.

Authentic Cadences.

103.

In Example 103, *a*, the common tone $\bar{g}$ is in the tenor part in
the dominant chord, and must therefore stay in the same part
in the tonic chord.

In Example 103, *b*, the common tone $\bar{\bar{g}}$ is in the soprano part
in the dominant chord, and must therefore stay in the same part
in the tonic chord.

In Example 103, *c*, the dominant chord has the leading tone in
the soprano part, which is led to the tonic in the soprano part of
the tonic chord. An ending is more complete when the tonic is
in the soprano part of the last chord. Therefore the cadence in
Example 103, *c*, is more complete than the cadences in Example 103, *a* and *b*.

In minor as well as in major keys a close formed by the succession of the dominant and tonic chords is an authentic
cadence.

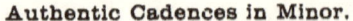

Authentic Cadences in Minor.

104.

a:V   I   g:V   I   d:V   I

Write authentic cadences in all the major and minor keys and practise playing them.

Exercise in Ear Training.

Play authentic cadences in major and minor keys. Let the pupil distinguish between them, at a distance from the piano.

CHAPTER XXI.

The Plagal Cadence.

A close formed by the subdominant chord followed by the tonic chord is called a **plagal cadence**.

Plagal Cadences.

The **subdominant** tone in the bass of a plagal cadence is led a skip of a fifth upward or a skip of a fourth downward to the **tonic** in the tonic chord.

In Example 105, *a*, the common tone in the subdominant and tonic chords is $\bar{\bar{c}}$. It is in the soprano part in the subdominant chord, therefore it must stay in the same part in the tonic chord.

In Example 105, *b*, the common tone in the subdominant and tonic chords is $\bar{g}$. It is in the soprano part in the subdominant chord, therefore it must stay in the same part in the tonic chord.

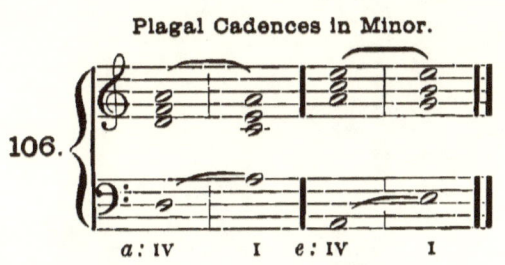

Plagal Cadences in Minor.

The subdominant and tonic chords in minor keys are minor chords. You must listen the next time you hear an Amen sung in church ; it is generally a plagal cadence.

Write plagal cadences in all the major and minor keys, and practise playing them.

Exercise in Ear Training.

Play plagal cadences in major and minor keys. Let the pupil distinguish at a distance from the piano whether they are in major or minor. Play authentic and plagal cadences, and let the pupil distinguish between them.

CHAPTER XXII.

Resolution of the Dominant Seventh Chord.

We have learned that an authentic cadence is the dominant chord followed by the tonic chord. When the cadence is formed by the dominant seventh chord followed by the tonic chord, the close is more complete, and is called a **perfect cadence.** Very often the perfect cadence is also called an authentic cadence.

Perfect Cadences.

107. $C:V_7$ I $C:V_7$ I $A:V_7$ I

In Example 107, in *a*, *b*, and *c*, the fifth of the dominant seventh chord has been left out. The fifth of the dominant seventh chord is very often omitted and the root doubled.

In the bass of the perfect cadence, the **root** of the dominant seventh chord is led a skip of a fourth upward or a skip of a fifth downward to the tonic in the tonic chord :

108. $C:V$ I $C:V$ I

The third and fifth of the dominant seventh chord progress according to the rules already given.

The **seventh** of the dominant seventh chord is led a half step downward to the third of the tonic chord :

109.

In major.

The **seventh** in the dominant seventh chord is the characteristic interval. It naturally falls to the nearest tone in the tonic chord. You can hear this if you play :

110.

In Example 110, *a*, the seventh has resolved a half step downward and your ear is satisfied, whereas in *b* the seventh having ascended leaves a sense of incompletion.

111.

Perfect Cadences.

F: V₇ I

In Example 111, the seventh of the dominant seventh chord, $\bar{b}\flat$, is led a half step downward to the third of the tonic chord.

The bass of the dominant seventh chord is led a skip upward to the tonic in the tonic chord.

The third of the dominant seventh chord, $\bar{e}$, the leading tone of the key, is led a half step upward to the tonic, while $\bar{g}$, the fifth of the dominant seventh chord, is led a whole step downward to the tonic in the tonic chord.

To become familiar with the resolution of the dominant seventh chord practise it as given in the following example:

112.

In Examples 112 and 113 the dominant seventh chords resolve into major chords (the tonic chords of major keys). The seventh of the dominant seventh chords is led a half step downward to the major third of the tonic chords.

In a minor key the seventh of the dominant seventh chord is led a whole step downward to the minor third of the tonic chord.

114.

We have said that the leading tone is led a half step upward to the tonic; there are exceptions to this rule. When the leading tone is in a **middle part**, in the alto or tenor, and when the bass moves in **contrary motion**, the leading tone may be led downward. Therefore Example 112, *a*, could be played thus:

115.

C: V₇   I

In Example 115 the leading tone, *b*, is in the tenor part, and is led downward to *g* in the tonic chord, while the bass moves upward to the tonic in contrary motion. In Example 115 the tonic chord is complete. In Example 112, *a*, the tonic chord is not complete; the leading tone in the dominant chord is led a half step upward to the tonic in the tonic chord, and thus the fifth in the tonic chord is omitted.

Example 114, *a*, could be played thus:

116.

a: V₇   I

The leading tone, g♯, is in a middle part, and the bass moves in contrary motion.

Write the dominant seventh chord followed by the tonic chord, as shown in Example 112, a, b, and c, in all major and minor keys.

Exercise in Ear Training.

Play perfect cadences in major and minor keys, and also play perfect, authentic, and plagal cadences. Let the pupil distinguish between these, not seeing the keyboard.

It will take the pupil two or three months to learn to play and to write the perfect cadence in all the major and minor keys. Try to teach him during this time to distinguish readily by ear the different cadences, not neglecting the exercises that have been given in the preceding chapters.

CHAPTER XXIII.

Diminished Seventh Chord.

All the triads built on the different degrees of the major and minor scales can have a seventh from the root (belonging to the same key) added to them. When a seventh from the root is added to a triad, the chord is called a **chord of the seventh.** All chords of the seventh are dependent chords and have to be resolved.

The principal or primary chord of the seventh is the dominant seventh chord. The other chords of the seventh are called secondary chords of the seventh.

A very important chord of the seventh is the **diminished seventh chord.** It is formed by adding a diminished seventh to the triad built on the seventh degree of the minor scale. It consists of a root, a minor third, a diminished fifth, and a diminished seventh :

$a:$ VII°

Build diminished seventh chords on A, G♯, F♯, B, B♭, D, F, etc.

The tones of a diminished seventh chord are the same distance from one another. Between the root and third there is a minor third ; between the third and fifth there is a minor third ; between the fifth and seventh, another minor third. The diminished seventh chord being built on the leading tone of a minor key resolves to the tonic chord of the minor key to which it belongs ; for the leading tone naturally ascends to the tonic, while the seventh of the chord as naturally falls or resolves to the fifth of the tonic chord.

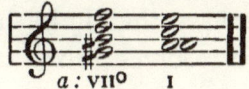

a: VII°   I

You will also find it resolving as well to the tonic chord
of the major key of the same name :

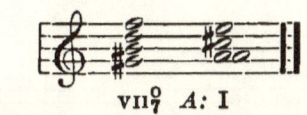

VII°₇   A: I

117.

c: VII°₇   I   VII°₇ C: I   d: VII°₇   I   VII°₇ D: I
            or   or

There are many other resolutions of the diminished seventh
chord. To study them here would take us too far. From this
chapter is to be learned the construction of the diminished
seventh chord, and the power to recognize it when heard.

The two passages below are from Mozart's " Fantasie" in *d*
minor. In Example 118 the diminished seventh chord built on f♯,
the leading tone of the scale of *g* minor, resolves to the tonic
chord of *g* minor :

118.

g : VII°₇

In Example 119* we have the diminished seventh chord built on the tone of g♯, which resolves to the tonic chord of A major.

Practise writing and playing diminished seventh chords.

Exercise in Ear Training.

Play diminished seventh chords; resolve them into major and minor chords. Let the pupil, at a distance from the piano, tell you whether you have resolved them into major or minor chords.

Play broken diminished seventh chords, and resolve them into broken major and minor chords.

CHAPTER XXIV.

The Secondary Chords of the Seventh in Major.

Chords of the seventh, as we have learned in the last chapter, can be built on any degree of the major or minor scale. They will differ, however, greatly from one another. We will first study the chords of the seventh in major.

Chords of the Seventh in Major.

The chords of the seventh on the **first** and **fourth** degree are alike in construction; they are major triads with major sevenths:

The chords of the seventh on the **second, third,** and **sixth** degree are alike in construction; they are minor triads with minor sevenths:

The chord of the seventh on the **seventh** degree is a diminished triad with a minor seventh:

The primary chord of the seventh is on the **fifth** degree. It stands alone as the only major triad with a minor seventh.

124.

$C: V_7$

There are **four different kinds** of chords of the seventh; as shown in Examples 121, 122, 123, 124, built on the different degrees of the major scale.

Write out the chords of the seventh built on the different degrees of the major scale in all the major keys.

Exercise in Ear Training.

Play the different chords of the seventh in major and let the pupil, not seeing the keyboard, try to distinguish between them.

CHAPTER XXV.

The Secondary Chords of the Seventh in Minor.

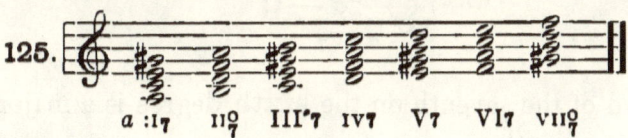

On examining the chords of the seventh in minor we find:

The chord of the seventh on the **first** degree is a minor triad with a major seventh:

The chord of the seventh on the **second** degree is a diminished triad with a minor seventh:

The chord of the seventh on the **third** degree is an augmented triad with a major seventh:

The chord of the seventh on the **fourth** degree is a minor triad with a minor seventh:

The primary chord of the seventh is on the **fifth** degree. It is the only major triad with a minor seventh.

130. *a*: V₇

The chord of the seventh on the **sixth** degree is a major triad with a major seventh :

131. *a*: VI₇

The chord of the seventh on the **seventh** degree is a diminished triad with a diminished seventh.

132. *a*: vii°₇

Each degree of the minor scale has a differently constructed chord of the seventh built on it; thus there are **seven different kinds** of chords of the seventh to be found in minor. Four chords of the seventh in minor, however, have the same construction as chords of the seventh in the major mode. Study the table on page 90.

Write the chords of the seventh built on the different degrees of the minor scale in all minor keys.

Exercise in Ear Training.

Let the pupil try to distinguish, not seeing the keyboard, between the different chords of the seventh in minor.

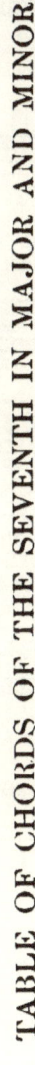

TABLE OF CHORDS OF THE SEVENTH IN MAJOR AND MINOR.

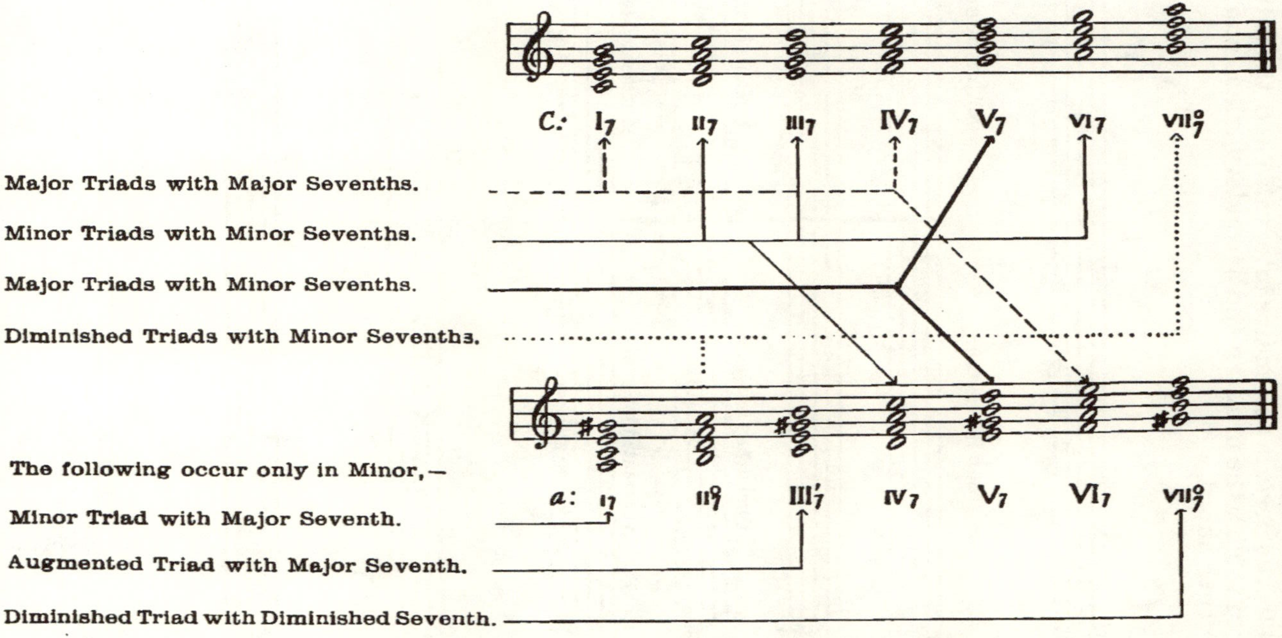

C: I_7 II_7 III_7 IV_7 V_7 VI_7 VII^o_7
Major Triads with Major Sevenths.
Minor Triads with Minor Sevenths.
Major Triads with Minor Sevenths.
Diminished Triads with Minor Sevenths.
The following occur only in Minor,—
a: I_7 II^o_7 III'_7 IV_7 V_7 VI_7 VII^o_7
Minor Triad with Major Seventh.
Augmented Triad with Major Seventh.
Diminished Triad with Diminished Seventh.

Write out, as shown in this table, in all major keys the major scale, the perfect and major intervals (and the intervals formed from them), the primary and secondary triads and the dominant seventh chord.

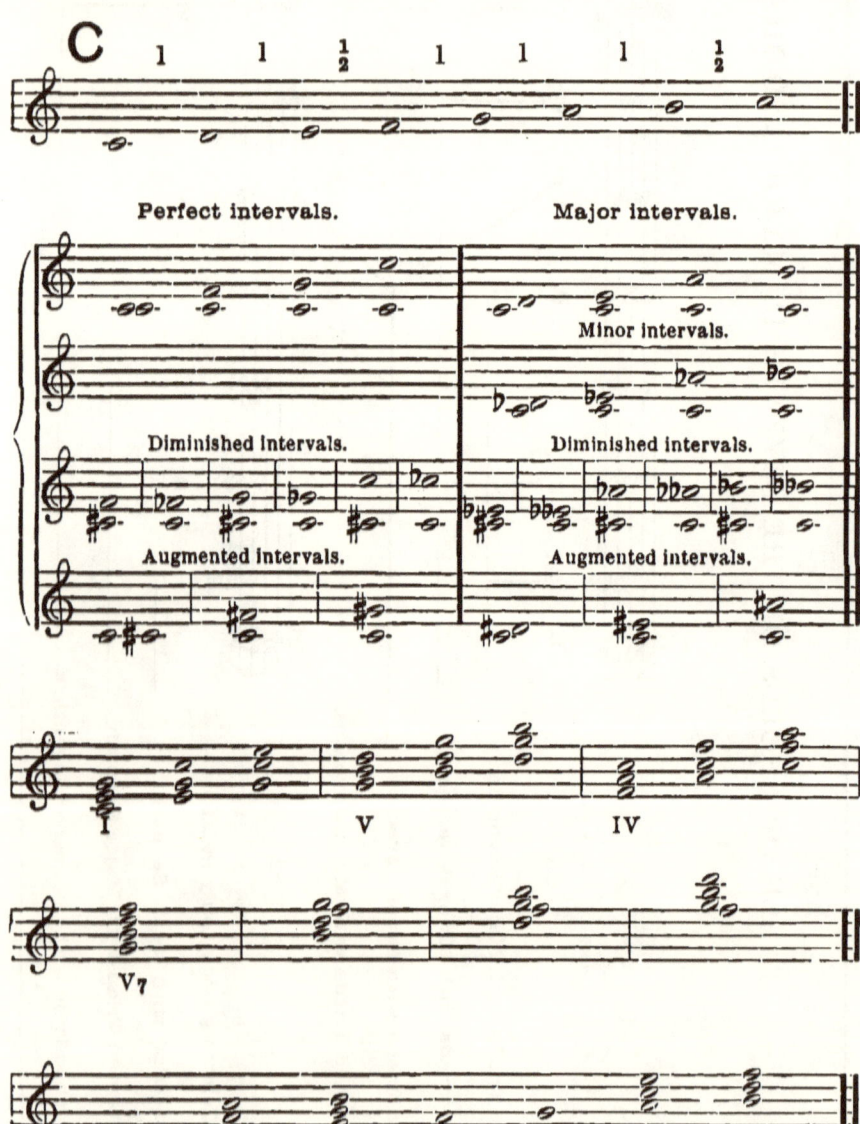

Write out, as shown in this table, in all minor keys the harmonic minor scale, the intervals reckoned from the tonic of each minor scale, the primary and secondary triads, the dominant seventh chord, and the melodic minor scale.

a minor.

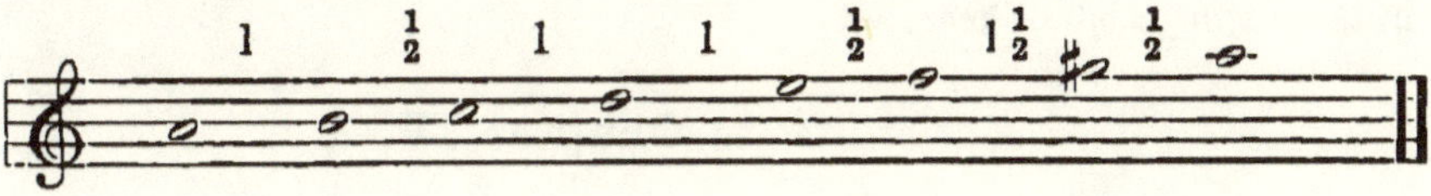

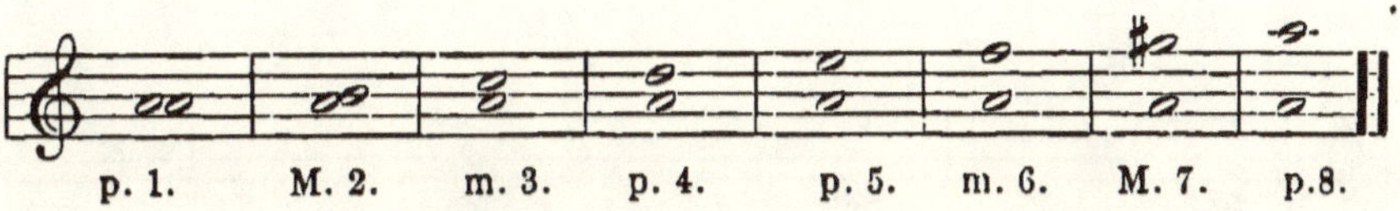

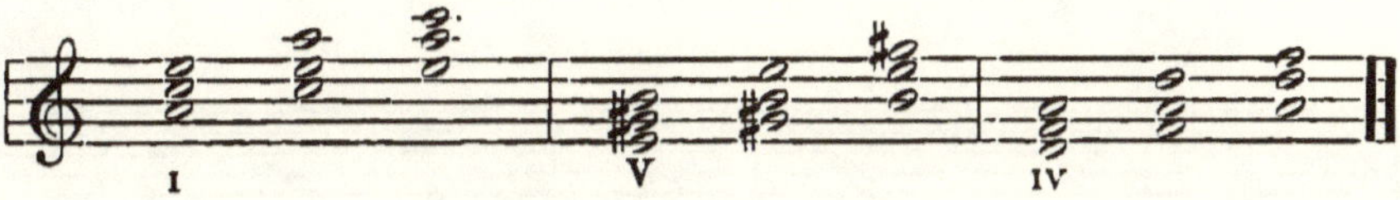

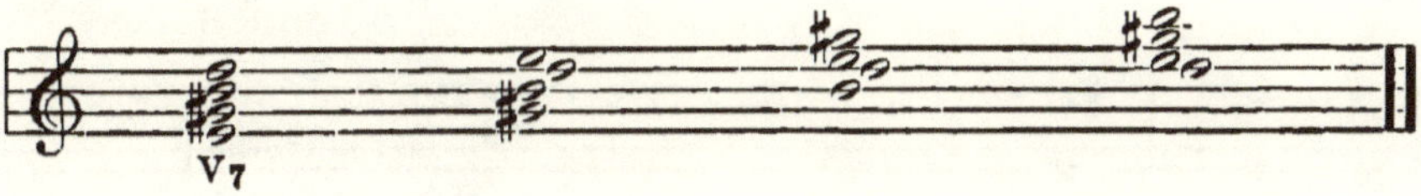

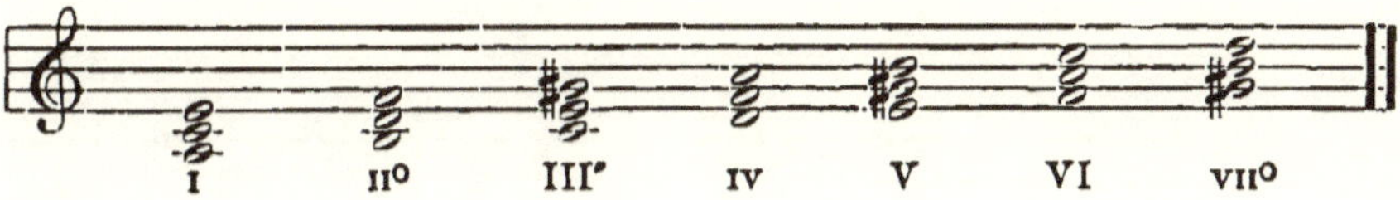

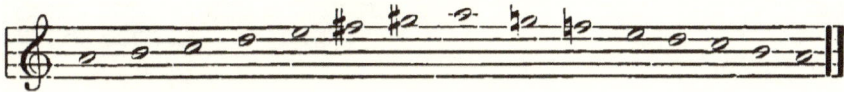

Melodic Minor Scale.

APPENDICES.

The exercise in the Appendix to a chapter is to be worked out by the pupil after he has written the intervals or chords, of which the chapter treats, in all the major or minor keys.

Appendix to Chapter IV.

Designate each interval as perfect or major; the perfect with p, the major with a capital M, and number each as a second, third, fourth, etc.

p. 4.   M. 3.   p. 8.

Appendix to Chapter V.

Designate the key to which each triad belongs and the degree on which it is built. When a triad is given several times in succession, designate it as belonging to as many different keys.

G: I   C: V   C: I   F: I

C : I   G : I   G : I   D : I

Appendix to Chapter VI.

Designate each interval as perfect major or minor, the minor
with a small m, and number each interval.

m. 7.   m. 3.

Write the notes forming the intervals indicated.

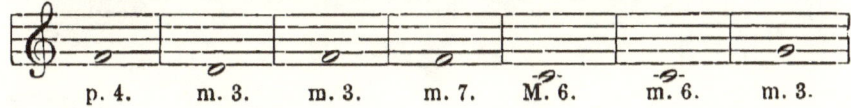

p. 4.   m. 3.   m. 3.   m. 7.   M. 6.   m. 6.   m. 3.

m. 7.   m. 7.   M. 2.   p. 5.   M. 3.   m. 3.   m. 6.

Designate each triad as major or minor.

Write the notes forming the triads indicated.

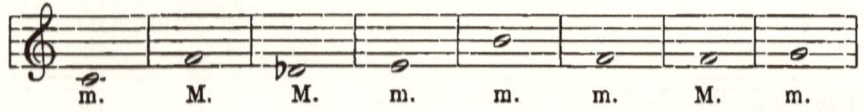

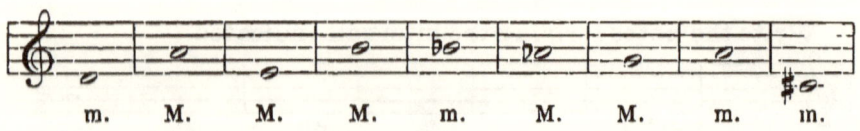

Appendix to Chapter VII.

Designate the key to which each dominant seventh chord belongs.

G :V₇   C :V₇   C :V₇

C: V₇

C: V₇

Appendix to Chapter VIII.

Designate each interval, diminished with d.

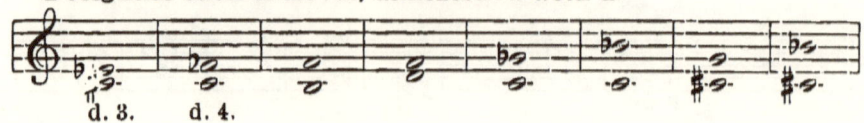

d. 3.   d. 4.

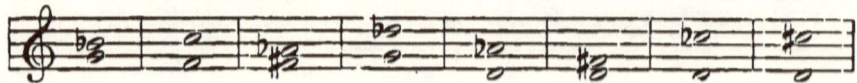

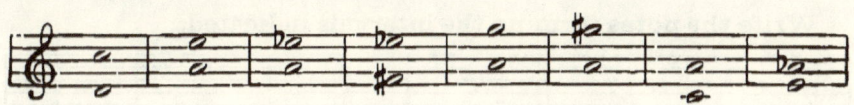

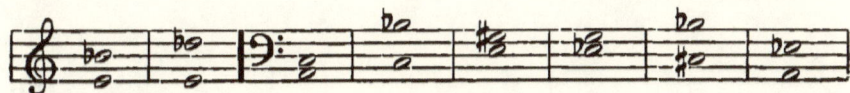

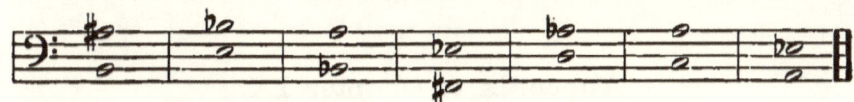

Reckon each interval from the bass note, and designate it.

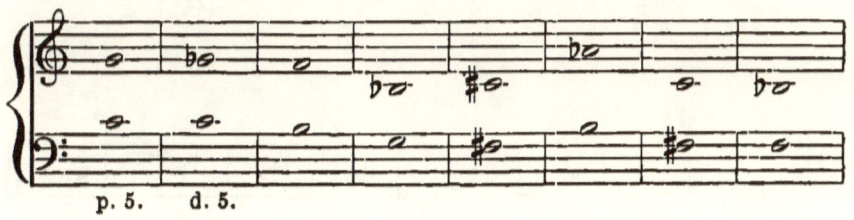

p. 5.　　d. 5.

Write the notes forming the intervals indicated.

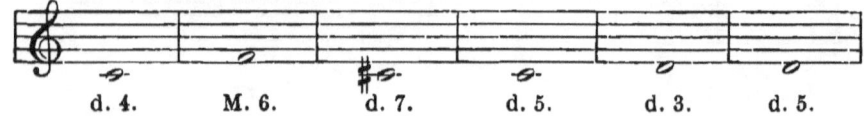

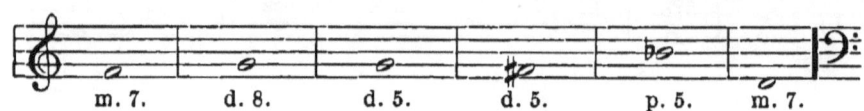

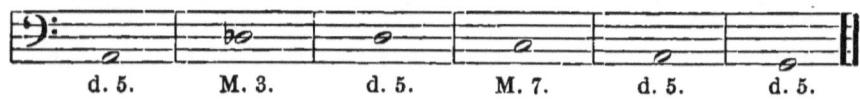

Appendix to Chapter IX.

Designate each interval, the augmented with a.

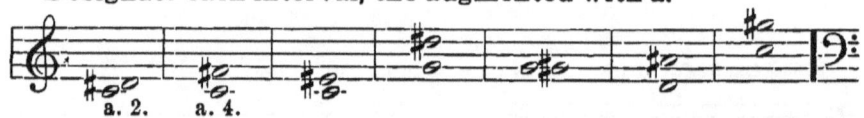

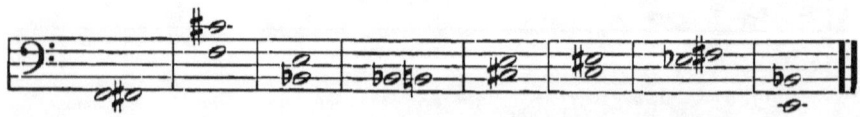

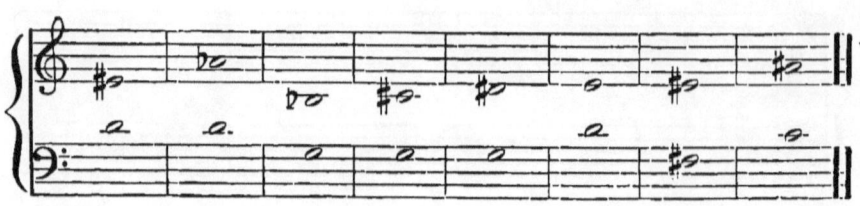

Write the notes forming the intervals indicated.

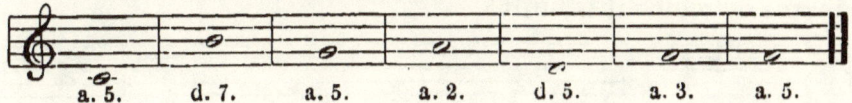

a. 5.   d. 7.   a. 5.   a. 2.   d. 5.   a. 3.   a. 5.

a. 5.   a. 2.   d. 8.   a. 5.   a. 5.   a. 6.   d. 7.

Appendix to Chapter X.

Write the notes forming the triads indicated.

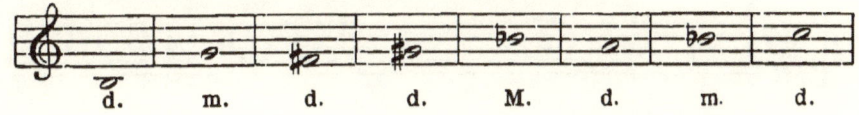

d.   m.   d.   d.   M.   d.   m.   d.

d.   m.   M.   d.   d.   d.   d.

d.   d.   m.   d.   M.   m.   d.

d.   d.   d.   M.   m.   d.   d.

Designate the major key to which each triad belongs, and the degree on which it is built.

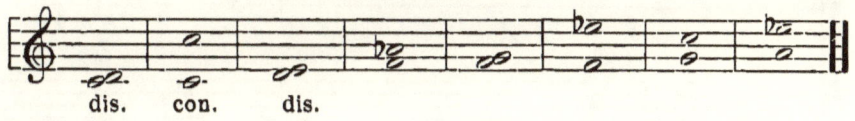

Appendix to Chapter XI.

Designate each interval as consonant or dissonant, the consonant with con., the dissonant with dis.

dis.   con.   dis.

Designate each chord as consonant or dissonant.

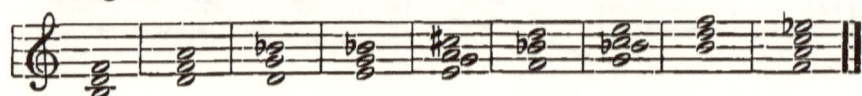

Appendix to Chapter XII.

Designate each interval, and write its inversion upon the staff below, and designate the inversion also.

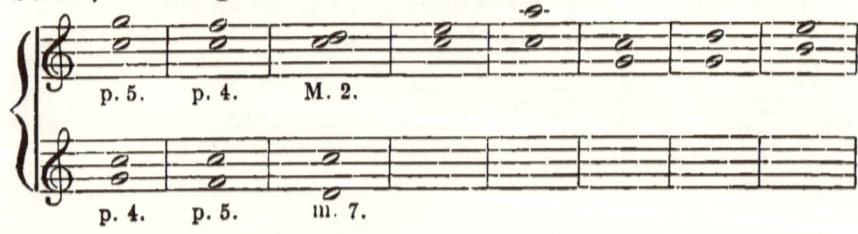

p. 5.   p. 4.   M. 2.

p. 4.   p. 5.   m. 7.

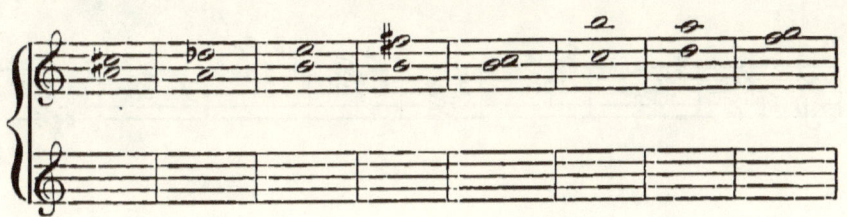

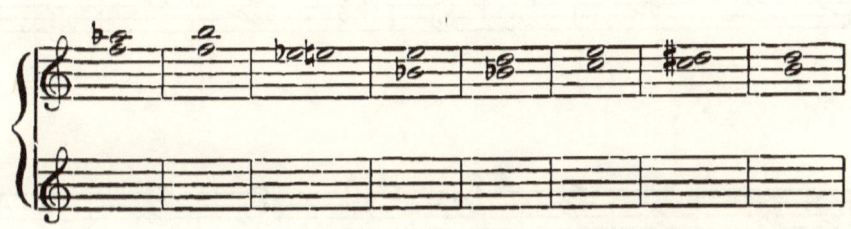

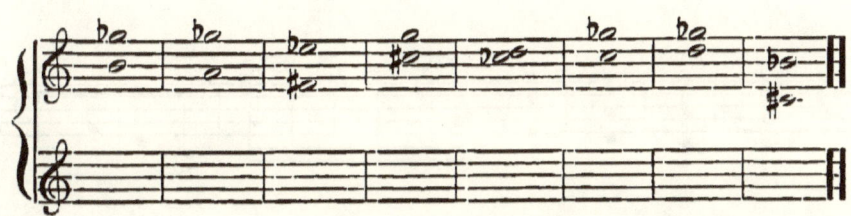

Appendix to Chapter XIV.

Designate the minor key to which each chord belongs, and the degree on which it is built. A minor key is designated by a small letter.

a. I.   a. V.

Appendix to Chapter XV.

Designate the minor key to which each chord belongs, and the degree on which it is built.

a: VI   e: III'   c: VII⁰

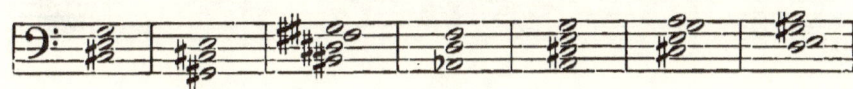

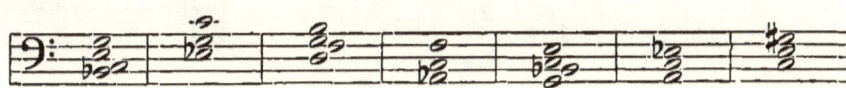

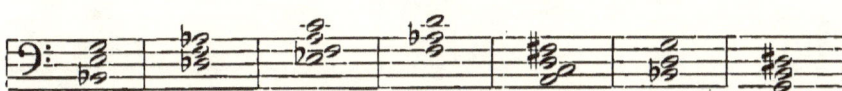

Appendix to Chapter **XXIV**.

Designate the key and the degree on which each chord is built.

C: II⁷   *C:* VII⁰₇   *F:* I₇

Appendix to Chapter XXV.

Designate the minor key and the degree on which each chord
is built.

www.ingramcontent.com/pod-product-compliance
Lightning Source LLC
Chambersburg PA
CBHW022142020726
47496CB00008B/2519